MW01626214

Made It!

Bernie Mulligan

Published by DD9 Publishing

ISBN-10: 0-9976818-1-0
ISBN-13: 978-0-9976818-1-9

First Edition.

Cover Design by Holly Emidy

Illustrations by *Emily McCoomb*

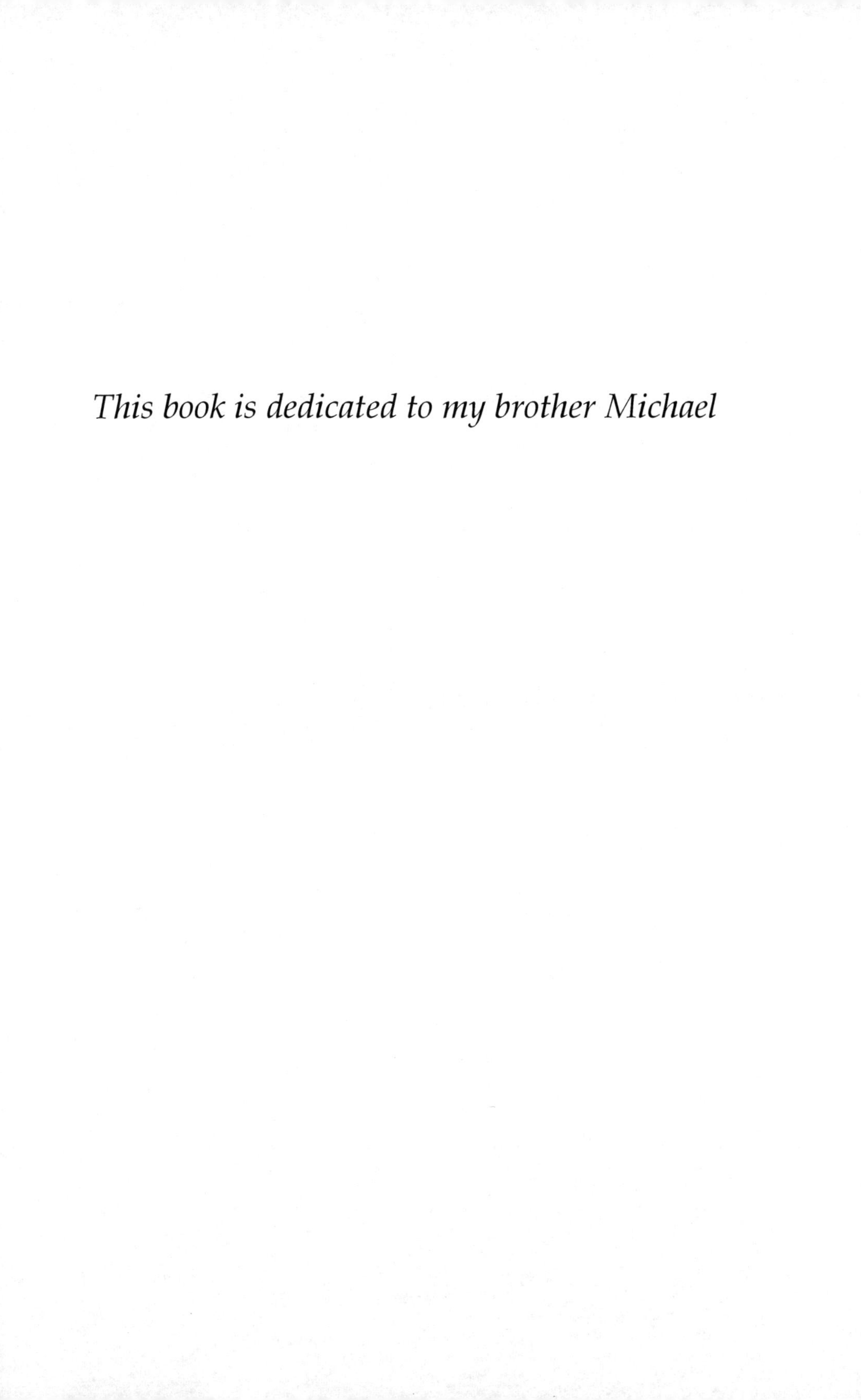

This book is dedicated to my brother Michael

Part One

Preface

Bernard with his sister, Mary Theresa

Dear Marie,

"I've come back to America with eyes very much more widely open- better able to see just what this country is like- almost as though I were a stranger, neutral, yet rather unkind. Its effect upon you is the thought uppermost in my mind right now. Recall the time we sat before the fireplace and I tried to dissuade you. Don't think I was being chivalrous but presenting the honest and necessary truth. You will know unhappy, perhaps bewildered moments, and all my love will not avail one whit. You will have many happy moments, too, my sweetheart. It seems I stand to gain far more than you. I don't care for that, but it is so. The future that lies before me is not an easy one- I'll need every reserve of will and effort to pull me through. I've confessed to you more than once my easy-going philosophy. 'Via est omnia.' The thing is to have a goal, not necessarily the attainment. It was an excellent system when I was alone. Now it is we and every decision I make from now on is not my own, it is yours and mine. This revolution within I don't mind admitting sometimes staggers me. One aspect always serves to busy me up. If you can face leaving lovely England, your mother, your father, Maurice, your friends, and most of all the familiar atmosphere you have become steeped in, your past, Oxford, the Lakes, Rosemary, your childhood, Lowther Road, the beach, theaters, music, school- all these things add up to your England, you must really love me. You will not really know the depth of your roots until you are uprooted, and actually what do I return for all this- only my love. It comes to that and no more, but my love is not the quiet, strong, steady affection that ought to be in keeping with my character- it is strong but turbulent and impatient."

- Bernard J. Mulligan

Chapter One - Marie

Marie Andree Cooper, England, 1937

Marie squinted as she scanned the horizon. The English Channel stretched out before her; a line of ships spewing black clouds of smoke moved slowly in the distance. She kicked off her sandals and slapped them together, returning sand to the beach. As she slipped them into the bag that was slung from her shoulder, the soles of her feet were massaged in the cool granules that crept up to her ankles. Marie reveled in a sense of hope that she had not felt in years —the bombing had gradually ceased, and the war seemed to have an end in sight. She pushed her wire-rimmed glasses up as tears smarted the creases of her eyes. She thought of the loss of her cat, Prudence, who had disappeared a year earlier during a particularly violent German air assault. "All the innocent animals that have passed away," she thought. Her throat ached with sadness.

Marie approached the tide pools, shimmering in the morning sun. She sat on a flat rock and rested her feet on the crest of a pool. The wind that tussled her wavy, auburn hair, disturbed the surface of the pool, distorting the life forms immersed there. The largest resident, a starfish, rested on the bottom surrounded by tufts of seaweed. When the wind diminished and the pool calmed, Marie could see that the starfish was missing two appendages. "Another casualty," she thought as she pulled it from the water. She held the starfish carefully. The creature was alive. "Seems that you'll have to get along," she chirped, smiling, before dropping it gently. The starfish descended slowly to the sandy bottom.

As she ambled down the beach, she felt around for the notebook. Emotions stirred in Marie at quiet moments like this. Thoughts of the war, her family, her pets, and her friends floated uneasily around her heart like the seaweed and debris being tossed in the surf. Touching the frayed corners of her notebook, she remembered the letter she had written to her good friend Hilde with whom she had bicycled around Germany in the summer of 1938. Marie plopped down on the sand, straightened her skirt, and found the unfinished letter in her notebook.

Dear Hilde, *September 15, 1943*

I am writing to you understanding full well that I will not risk sending this letter. I will speak to you but you shall not listen nor shall you hear. Even as the bombing subsides in England it is increasing in Germany. I am in fear for you, my dearest friend. England's survival, its victory, and Germany's defeat, while these are my fervent hope they are my dread. I cannot bear to lose you. This horrible war; its consequences; the destruction of innocents, the decimation of the landscape, and the distance it imposes on us, all these things erode my faith. Last week, I emerged from the shelter to the sight of a black and red streaked sky. A vertical length of plumbing protruded from the rubble and a dripping toilet was dangling from its apex. Such is the horrendous absurdity of war…..

The afternoon sun sunk behind the fog as it enveloped the passing ships, portending an early and chilly end to the day. Marie slid the notebook back into the bag and retreated up the cement stairs to the boardwalk and the folding cabanas towards the streets of Bournemouth.

***

Marie Andree Cooper, was born June 17th, 1917, to Jasper and Andree Cooper in Bournemouth England. Jasper Cooper was an entrepreneur, building vehicles for the Russian and English military. His company also manufactured motor cars for racing and leisure. Marie, and her much older brother, Maurice, grew up privileged. The Cooper household was kept clean by maids and they both attended the best schools. Her childhood diaries are filled with brochures of high school plays and postcards from hotels where the Cooper family stayed on their travels. Frequently, they would cross the English Channel to visit Paris where my Jasper Cooper had business interests.

From birth, Marie spoke only French because she lived with her mother and it was intended that she be multilingual. Initially, having English as a second language caused some difficulties at school. At 7 years of age she became proficient in English as well as French. She and her mother always spoke in French, excluding Jasper Cooper from the conversation until he would clear his throat and say in exasperation; "Ahem, speak English, please."

Her mother, Andree, whom everyone called Meme, was a strong character with a clear idea of class. She was polite, but very cynical. She felt that there was a specific way to behave at a dinner table, and in fact, a predetermined means of deportment for every situation. She also believed that one should look their best no matter how scant their resources. Marie was a Protestant, but Meme was an Atheist, and thus faith was never an important part of life for their family except as a topic of debate. This was unusual for the time, since religion was the source of consolation for many who lived through the horrendous bombing of England. Meme had been a nurse during World War I, and the barbarism of war only deepened Meme's belief that God did not exist and that humans were weak and cruel. Marie's religious training was given only as a concession to her father, who felt that it helped build character. Marie did believe in God, but this belief was not intense, and certainly she did not think about it very much. Her true belief was in the fundamental goodness of her fellow human beings. When Meme would criticize people, as she often did, Marie would cringe and try to explain the foible or bad behavior as an unfortunate result of some malady or psychological trauma.

In 1938, at age 21, Marie travelled to Germany to visit her dear friend Hilde and to practice her German. She and Hilde rode their bicycles all over Germany into the Black Forest and along the Rhine. Hitler was ranting on the radio, but neither Hilde nor Marie talked about the political state of Germany. They were relatively apolitical, and like the German people, believed that the new regime had brought financial stability and a relief from the inflation they had endured during the Weimar Republic. Yet, neither could fully ignore the increased burden of government scrutiny as they travelled. My mother returned to England and continued her studies. The invasion of Poland by Germany the following year was devastating to her, because she knew that the national socialists would close down communication with England, just as surely as she knew that England would reciprocate. She did not communicate with Hilde until the war ended, and by then both had matured and aged. Hilde and Marie corresponded all their lives by letter or Western Union, always written in German.

War brought rationing, destruction, and fear to England, fought by the uplifting pep talks of Winston Churchill. The German rockets would announce their imminent drop with the sudden cessation of their droning, razing buildings and cratering the English countryside. The people were kept in a constant state of anxiety with the harshest reality of war—death—looming above them. For my mother, the strangeness of a dead classmate that she had barely become acquainted with, the death of an animal that she'd seen on her walk, or the sudden disappearance of a city block, brought her naivete to an abrupt end. Suddenly, death was tangible--causing her to realize that the family and friends that she loved could be speaking to her one day, and be broken and buried in rubble the next. However, she did not hate the Germans like her mother and father did. She believed that it was Hitler and his sycophants that dropped the bombs, not the people she met while riding her bicycle along the Rhine. She feared for her friend Hilde, but she avoided thinking about it, because there would be no way of knowing if she survived. Marie was a complicated personality. Sometimes her approach to tragedy could be astonishingly brave and steadfast, willing to face any horror to empathize or assist those in need. At other times, she felt brittle and weak and fell to pieces thinking about the smallest details she observed as by-products of war, the skeletons of bombed houses and the dead promises of a farmer's abandoned field.

Cooper Family, 1920

Chapter Two - Bernard

He dips his pen in starry wells
This poet, scholar, seer:
In roaming vales and moonlight dells
Our Bern's without a peer.
--St. Mary Academy Yearbook Poem
By Classmates 1935

Bernard John Mulligan 8 years old

Bernard stared out the bedroom window; autumn leaves were twitching in the gusty morning breeze. The dawn arrived in a deliberate way this morning. The sky had brightened methodically, almost imperceptibly and slowly illuminated the features of his room. The chessboard, bookcase, crucifix, and radio presented their familiar faces for his contemplation. He sighed as he pushed off the sheets and blanket and walked intently to his desk. The entry he had crafted at two A.M. that morning stared up at him from his little leather notebook.

It becomes a cast of mind and so it seems I have been a sergeant all my life. It began with Pearl Harbor while I was a pin fold machine operator during the night, a gluteal biology student during the day, a very moderate drinker, and an inept pursuer of females in the evening. My needs for sleep were mostly satisfied during zoology and organic chemistry, as my transcript will testify.

He placed the book down gently on the desk and pulled a pressed white shirt out of the closet. The stiff cotton felt foreign and unwanted as he slid his arms into the starched sleeves. He stared at himself in the mirror and quickly sat down again, grasping the pen:

I have always wanted to write diaries. And yet, my last act before going into the army March 1943 was to burn four fat ones in the old coal stove. So many interesting things happen even on a dull day that it is a crime not to record them.

There was always a compelling sense that his view of the world needed explanation, even for him, to understand. Someday, he secretly hoped that someone would find his carefully hidden volumes.

Mostly, the interior of my cranium is a muddle, a ceaseless play of colors, restless pictures, moods, feelings. Thought should be an orderly process or sequence of ideas. My thoughts are not orderly. When I think, I am peering down into a large turbulent kettle where, occasionally, I glimpse bits of the truth.

Bernard let the pages fan gently across his fingertips as the diary closed. Sinking into the chair, he cradled the back of his neck with clasped hands. His destinations, his appointments, and his duties of the day had faded as he absorbed himself in the contemplation of his life and the recording of his deeds. The morning sun intensified, filling his room with brilliant light, and flooding his mind again with a tumult of responsibility.

***

Bernard John Mulligan, was born November 14th, 1916. He was the first child in an Irish Roman Catholic family from Meadville, Pennsylvania, where his father, James Mulligan, was a plumber. His mother, Luella Mulligan, was a strong woman of conviction who stayed at home and attended to her children: Bernard, Joseph, James, Edward, and Mary Theresa. In Meadville in the 1930's, one either worked for the railroad or worked in the town's various little factories. Everyone farmed. Cornfields were abundant. These farming activities supplemented the income derived from the work in the factories, stores, and from the railroad.

His mother had been a hand model in her youth for a dress fastener company and had also modeled clothing, but she certainly did not have the disposition or the face of a model. She was tough and she firmly believed that idle hands are the "devil's workshop"; she always stayed very busy. Luella was a strict mother, but also kind, with a keen sense of humor. Her hair was red and unruly, she mostly wore slippers, and her apron had many pockets filled with wooden spoons and other cooking tools. She cooked large meals on the cast iron stove and delighted guests with her tasty apple pie. Every child was expected to attend the meals, commencing with Grace; Sunday dinner, especially, was as much of an obligation as Confession.

Corporal punishment was also typical at home, and Luella Mulligan could inflict swift justice if you acted up at the table.

Until the Great Depression, James Mulligan had owned his own plumbing shop on Arch Street. His good customers would receive leather-bound dictionaries as gifts for their loyalty. Although he held patents and was a good plumber, the depression hurt him financially. He wanted to make sulfur springs more accessible through plumbing and his patents attended to this goal. At the time, many people bathed in the numerous, warm, lime springs in Upstate New York and Northwestern Pennsylvania. The idea fizzled, and his many hours of hard work were squandered. He also trusted people, and because of that, he was occasionally taken advantage of especially when he loaned people money, but often did not have the heart to collect. He did not spend a lot of time with his children, but he made it clear to them that school was important.

Bernard's childhood was happy. He loved sports, and although he worked diligently at his schoolwork, he did not become obsessed with it. There were many diversions for children growing up in Meadville, and one of his favorites was swimming. French Creek, his preferred swimming hole, is a large, fast-moving river that splits the town right down the middle. It offered bridges for diving, and the fast current added to the fun. Most Meadville children's rite of passage was to swim the width of Conneaut Lake. Bernard swam across the lake first and his brothers soon followed. When the Mulligan family took trips to Lake Erie, 40 miles north, they had picnics on Presque Isle's beaches, and the waves of the lake added a new challenge to the children's swimming skills. He and his siblings were kept well entertained--country fairs would arrive every summer, hay rides in the fall, and sledding all winter. He once told me that when he was a child he dreaded the prospect of growing up.

When Bernard reached high school, he became interested in music and languages. Piano practice, Latin, and incessant reading consumed him. He had developed an internal dialogue that he rarely shared with other people, but he was not shy, and he conversed with everyone who was willing. He always had a sharp wit and when he laughed, he bellowed. His private laughter was quiet; he reserved it for the endless ignorance he encountered, and for the irony that he witnessed throughout his lifetime.

Bernard was also deeply religious. The mystery of Mass and the Sacraments intrigued him so much that he studied Latin in order to understand the language of the Catholic Church. He went on to attend the Seminary in New York to become a priest, but he had a difficult time fitting in. When he came back from the Seminary, he became reclusive and he stayed in his room for more than a year while his mother took care of him. He became very proficient at chess and would play with visitors for hours. He was introverted, complex, and deeply emotional, and although he fought this tendency to be controlled by his emotions, it nonetheless proved to be a source of turmoil. His sense of isolation at the Seminary, coupled with the impending vows of celibacy and poverty, were too much of a commitment, given that he adored women and had many female friends. He gave them books with humorous or poignant salutations on the inside cover and he would tease them, but always in a complimentary way. He was unwilling to commit his life to the contemplative study of the priesthood, if that meant he would never experience the intimacy of marriage.

He joined the army two years after he left the Seminary. His brother Ed also joined and became a journalist, and soon Jim followed. Joe enlisted, but was sent home after basic training because of a crooked arm. Brother Jim died in the Pacific at Bougainville, one month before he was to return home. He died rescuing a fallen comrade, for which he received a Silver Star and a Purple Heart. The Mulligan family was devastated by this loss. When his sister, Mary Theresa, joined the convent, she took the name Sister James Francis as a tribute to her brother. Jim had been the most mischievous and yet the most charming of the boys. Bernard found it very difficult to talk about his younger brother and the topic of his death rarely came up. The Silver Star and Purple Heart that he earned became a shrine on a little round oak table in the household's living room. Unlike Jim, Bernard never saw combat, as he became a lab technician and was stationed in England. He was skilled in his position and he received written praise from his superiors. He tested milk and other perishable food for bacteria. Whenever anyone in his family or his close circle of friends became sick they heeded Bernard's advice because he understood biology so well.

Chapter Three - Romance

Picnic Marie and Bernard

During World War II, while he was stationed in England, Bernard met Marie in Bournemouth, a tourist town on the south shore of England. The Isle of Wight can be seen from the beach, and storms that batter the coast in the spring can be viewed long before they arrive. In the summer, people stroll up and down the beach, meeting with friends or sauntering around the boardwalk. Marie was wading through the wake of the sea as it smoothed the sand at the Bournemouth shore, when she saw a man sitting on a green army blanket, smoking a pipe, and reading books about music. She was so intrigued that she asked him about the music he was studying. Bernard was startled by the slim woman with wavy auburn hair but the topic of music placed him on firm ground. It was evident that she was equally passionate on the subject, though her favorite music differed from his. They talked for over an hour and she invited him to her home, where she lived with her brother, to meet her group of friends. She wanted to hear him play. He attended, and his piano playing won him immediate acceptance.

Over the ensuing months their compatibility, buoyed by their shared love of music, walks on the beach, and pints of ale in the pub, gained momentum. While their attraction deepened, they enjoyed endless debate and discussions. They were mentally well-matched and surrounded by enough history and culture for a constant source of conversation. Marie was faced with a complex man with formidable intellectual skill. Conversely, Bernard was breathlessly captivated by Marie's engagement in his discussion. They debated religion, politics, music, and literature passionately. She challenged him to defend his beliefs. In particular, she forced him to explain his Roman Catholic viewpoint. He knew he could not dodge or equivocate because she was an intellectual peer. They listened intently to one another. The intensity of their discourse pushed the communication beyond mere words. Facial expression and body language were observed and understood. Humor could temper the serious nature of their debate if a consensus could not be reached.

Neither had met anyone as intriguing as the other. The reminders of the bombing of Britain and the preparation for the D-Day invasion going on all around them did not deter their exploration of one another.

During the time that Marie was getting acquainted with Bernard, the bombing had begun to subside. Because her father was becoming wealthy and successful building war vehicles, the family could afford to buy rationed items on the black market. They enjoyed access to all the gasoline, butter, and coffee that their money provided. Meme was not particularly pleased by their relationship, but she showed restraint on voicing her opinion because of Bernard's obvious intelligence and considerable charm. Nonetheless, Meme knew that she could lose her only daughter to the United States, where the people cooked with lard and butchered the English language. Jasper Cooper's emotions on the subject were more reserved. He worked constantly and his spare time was consumed by photography, travel, and the new wireless radio that he had assembled in the spare room. However, when Marie and Bernard decided to get married, he wrote the following letter on his own letterhead:

Jasper Cooper
Member Institution Naval Architects
134 West Kensington Court
Consulting Engineer
London, W. 14
Examining Engineer-Royal Automobile Club

20 February 1946

My Dear Bernard,

Within a few days Marie will be on her way to you and placing on your shoulders the immense responsibility of supplying the mental, physical and emotional needs of that miracle of creation – a woman. Your woman happens also to possess an uncommon combination of qualities; she has great mental ability, more than the usual supply of loyalty and sincerity in her love and affection added to a strong, straightforward character.

If that does not frighten you, then you are worthy of the task and I would like to say that I have complete faith that your character will stand the test and that, between you, you will plough a steady course through the rough pastures of life,

I am alone in this London flat - Marie and her mother are at Dartmouth – but I speak for my wife as well as myself when I conclude by wishing you both a full, a happy and a useful life added to what is the greatest test of marriage, lifelong mutual confidence and help.

With my kindest regards and wishes
Your affectionate Father-In-Law to be

Jasper Cooper

In time, Meme warmed to Bernard. One could not ignore the young couples' compatibility. Meme seemed pleased that Marie's other suitors had fallen by the wayside. In her usual direct and uncompromising form she demonstrated her empathy for him with a scathing assessment of one of Marie's former suitors:

"Poor you, you must have had some painful times if you fell in love with Marie from the first. She was a long time discovering her own feelings! Anyway you are sure of her now. Dennis struck me as a very selfish young man and I think it was his self-pity and the want of pity from others which first attracted Marie as she is always ready to help the lame dog."

Prior to leaving England, Bernard had proposed and Marie was thinking it over. He had just mailed a ring to her in order to force a decision. He also had made a promise to bring her back to England from time to time in order to see her family, but there was never any question that she was going to America. English cities still showed the visible scars of the bombing, and rationing was an everyday hindrance. America had little rationing and was physically unscathed by the war. Another more important factor concerned gender expectation, for although Marie's education far exceeded Bernard's, his career was the only one being discussed. Marie wanted to have children eventually, but she also wanted to write and study. "I don't fancy just being a wife," she wrote.

Marie endured the long boat ride across the Atlantic and Bernard had made the trip by car from Meadville to New York to pick her up. He found her sitting on her luggage, waiting. He gathered her up and they drove back to Meadville so that he could introduce her to the family. After a short visit, they hastily drove to Indianapolis where they were married on March 11, 1946. Basking in the excitement of their new marriage. They packed up their car, Matilda, and drove into the Adirondacks for a six week honeymoon that summer.

Chapter Four - Adventures

Marie, Adirondack Mountains, NY, 1947

Bernard and Marie drove to the Adirondacks for the rest of their honeymoon. In their old 1939 Buick, with their beloved dog, Robin, at their side, they cruised around the National Forest's lakes and mountains. Throughout their six week trip in the mountains they kept a shared journal, and took many photographs.

Their travels took them to Lake Placid and Blue Mountain Lake, and they also camped at the Ausable River Chasm. On a night near Tupper Lake, as they dipped their feet in a stream, Marie slid her fingers under her new husband's palm. "I do so love driving with you. Every little town, every mountain, and each stream we see offers surprise and possibility. The problems we encounter are so often easy to solve with a meal, a good night's sleep, or a petrol station. I wish I could capture my thoughts as we drive for hours, pondering, but they seem a bit out of the realm of language. When we are driving I don't feel compelled to speak, but it's never awkward."

Marie glanced at Bernard. His eyes glistened as he replied, "Are you telling me to be quiet?" He laughed as he gripped his pipe. Marie released her grip and sunk her hands in the stream forming a cup. Pulling the water out of the stream, she poured it into Bernard's pipe. "Yes dear, would you?"

As they rattled down a dirt road the next morning, Bernard noticed a conspicuous noise coming from the back of Matilda. Listening, they discovered that something near the rear end was damaged. They drove far enough into civilization to use a phone and arrange for a tow to Lake Placid.

They continued camping in the National Forest while they waited for the car to be repaired. They hiked the nearby mountains, swam in the Ausable River, and basked in the occasional light of sun. A churning fog greeted them as they opened the flap on their tent on the day they were to retrieve the car. Robin stared at Marie, his tail wagging excitedly. Marie scratched his back and nudged him into a playful mood. "Oh yes, I will feed you and after we collect the car we will take you on a hike. Yes, yes, we will!"

With the use of Matilda again, they spent the following days canoeing, swimming, and hiking. On a clear, warm day they hiked

Mount Pitchoff. The summit promised a fantastic view of Mt. Cascade, directly across the valley and rising above Adirondack Lake. Awestruck at the top, and exhausted from many hours of climb, they laid on a large stone ledge to relax. Bernard realized that it would be dark soon. "We'd better get moving, dear," he whispered. He whistled for Robin who came bouncing out of the bushes. As they descended the mountain trail, they heard a rustling noise and Robin darted into the brush towards the source of the sound. He ignored Bernard's urgent whistles and Marie's commands to stop. They ran after Robin, but lost sight of him. Suddenly, a series of blood curdling yelps came from far in the distance.

Finally, they found their pet—whimpering and injured. "All I could imagine was that he was being torn apart by a mountain lion," Bernard later wrote in his diary. A quick inspection revealed that the dog had pounced on a porcupine and was impaled on his leg and paw. Bernard and Marie pulled out almost all of the quills except for two or three in his paw before continuing their descent, slowly assisting Robin along the trail to the car in the darkness. Frustrated and tired, they could not find a vet in Lake Placid. They drove on, comforting Robin as he whimpered in the back, until they found someone in Saranac Lake. The vet pulled out the quills, and treated the dog for mange and fleas acquired in the forest.

The rest of their trip passed quietly, and made a happy impression on them. Bernard eventually received his orders from the Army. The newlyweds moved into the family housing in Odenton, Maryland, and Bernard Mulligan was promoted to Sergeant. He began working in a hospital laboratory. At night Bernard and Marie listened to music, sipped beer, and dreamed of the future. Marie returned to England once in 1947, and described her feelings in a letter home:

My friends have changed; marriage, careers, and children dominate their existence. They have time for tea with an old friend like me, but that is the extent of it. I will miss my mother most of all but I am ready for my return to the states and you, my darling.

OUR COSY TENT

Chapter Five - Family Life

Mulligan Family, 1954
(left to right: Bernie, Marie, Patrick, Bernard, Michael)

In 1948, Michael John Mulligan was born while Bernard was still in the army. The new family lived in army housing; in a long line of drab units with tree-less yards and uneven sidewalks. Michael presented a stressful challenge for the new parents, and when Bernard returned from the lab she was frequently waiting in the doorway of the apartment, anxious to be relieved so that she could go for a walk or read a book. In the diaries, Bernard announced every new development: Michael's first step, his first unsupervised deposit into the commode, and his first sensible utterance. He said "ba ba" when he wanted his bottle. It did not take him long to learn the word; "no." Marie believed he would say no to reasonable requests and then relish her angry response. Two and a half years after Michael, Bernard Francis, called Bernie, was born at Fort Meade, Maryland, just prior to his father's honorable discharge. There is no mention of Bernie's step, first bathroom visit, or his discovery of speech in his diaries. Bernard wrote very little between 1948 and 1953.

Their lives, like the lives of many young couples escaping from the shadow of World War II, held so much promise. Bernard sought to complete his education on the GI Bill, while Marie took care of Michael and me. She worked part-time at the local colleges and at libraries. In 1953, they were still living in Odenton, Maryland, when he left for Brown University in Providence, RI, to study for his Masters Degree in Biology.

He attended his first semester there and my mother dutifully stayed behind, watching us. She dragged us to church and fed us well, but according to her letters we were often sick. Bernard attributed it to the well water, which he suspected was contaminated. This time was a difficult one for their marriage. Marie did not enjoy infants much, especially when they were crying or filling their diaper. Bernard, however, seemed to enjoy the exploration of Providence and the Brown campus and he faithfully detailed his escapades to Marie in his letters. It is clear that she envied his freedom. They wrote to each other three to four times per week, and she emphasized her frustration in her letters. One day without notice, Marie called her husband at his lab.

"I am very unhappy," she blurted into the phone. Bernard's heart jumped as she lashed out before he could say a word to address her. "How can you leave me here with these two children with no money and living in an army housing unit?" Bernard did not want to share his personal problems with his coworkers. "It seems to me that you find it very easy to compromise my happiness while you go out and conquer the world!" she continued. Bernard cringed. He whispered into the phone, "I can attend to this, and I will tonight, I promise." "Well!" Marie replied. " I suppose two intelligent people can work anything out." That night, he wrote a heartfelt letter:

I hope by the time you receive this, you will be feeling better. You sounded so unhappy on the phone and also your voice sounded stopped up as though your sinuses were giving you a bad time. Please don't let single sentences tell the whole story. Qualification is almost always necessary. You must know that your happiness is very close to my heart and if I must outgrow my distaste for housework, that I certainly will do. You say that two intelligent people can work things out and I think that that is certainly true. I didn't marry you with the purpose of making you unhappy or of demanding all these sacrifices without returns. When we are here together I will do all in my power to help make life satisfying for you.

Eventually, Bernard found a suitable home; a yellow and brown shingled cape on Ruth Avenue, built on what had once been a dump. Marie happily joined him in Rhode Island soon thereafter. They were so happy to be together again and to find their new house in Phillipsdale, a neighborhood in East Providence. Phillipsdale had been an independent town in the 1880's, with its own police station, firehouse, and barber shop. The town supported the needs of Washburn Wire, a huge wire plant on the banks of the Providence River. Like many New England towns, the homes there were built by the factory to house the workers. These houses near the plant were brick duplexes erected close to the banks of the Providence River and the noisy railroad tracks. Our street, Ruth Avenue, was on a hill above the duplexes, and the houses on Ruth Avenue were single family homes made of wood. Our house had been built in 1951. At this time, the city of East Providence had enveloped Phillipsdale and also the towns of Rumford, Kent Heights, and Riverside. As the area changed, the police department became a laundromat and a store, and the fire department became a private home.

The population of Phillipsdale was a mix of Portuguese and Irish families who worked at the local manufacturing sites. Being predominantly Catholic, the neighborhood eventually filled up with children. In 1954, my parents contributed another son, Patrick, to the swelling tide of children. In the evening families would congregate out on their front yards or steps drinking beer and socializing. Marie was inspired to write a quixotic poem about this scene and Bernard wrote a cynical sequel:

Summer Evening by *Marie Mulligan*

Soft summer dusk
Drives out the sweltering sun
Bringing coolness to the cheek,
Muting the raucous noise of the day.

Neighbors stand in twos and threes
Talking, leaning on lawn mowers,
Watering the yard, bringing in
The last of the day's wash.
Children dart about, quieter now,
Escaping bedtime, clutching
Sticky nickels for ice cream.

Now the night is warm and still,
A porch swing creaks nearby,
Quiet voices murmur, beer cans chink,
Giggling teenagers flirt

Around the neighborhood store.
Outside our house, the street light
Pierces the foliage of an elm's
Sunlit leaves

Our Street *by Bernard J. Mulligan*

Up and down our street,
The air is very sweet,
After the rubber mill
Is closed on the hill.

The children all chant aloud
About a bright green cloud,
Which finally blows away,
To end a bilious day.

Fathers and also mothers
Are full of bothers,
Baby is extremely happy,
Smudging his nappy.

Marty comes with jingling bell,
His frozen junks to sell,
Kids' dimes he quickly takes
In change for bellyaches.

Mummy sips his beer
While daddy calls her dear,
And off they go to bed
Much more drunk than wed.

Bernard continued to take biology and bacteriology classes at Brown University. Michael and Bernie played in the woods across the street from the house and interacted with the many children roaming the neighborhood. Two and a half months after Patrick was born, Marie became pregnant with David.

In 1955, everything seemed almost just right. Sure, there was a nuclear bomb, but Ike was at the helm and would protect us. America had just invented the transistor and radios became smaller and more portable. Bernard purchased a Philco Television in 1953 for $100.00, and even though it needed new tubes every once in a while, it offered hours of free entertainment with shows like *Gunsmoke, Palladin,* and *Howdy Doody*. The families on the TV all seemed happy. Dennis the Menace and Beaver had Moms in dresses with aprons, and they lived in beautiful homes. Their cars always started and there were no derelicts in their neighborhoods. Neither injury, illness, nor financial problems plagued anyone. No one on any of these shows contracted polio.

Even though the car broke down frequently, draining money and making them late, the Mulligans were a happy family. Marie walked her children in strollers on the new cement sidewalks of the town, stopping to talk and laugh with the other mothers in the neighborhood. It seemed as if children were being born every day. Then one day, a telegram shattered Marie's sense of domestic homeostasis.

Jasper Cooper died in June of 1955 of a heart attack. Marie's pregnancy made a trip home to England impossible, so she grieved at Ruth Avenue. She was often distracted by the needs of her three children and her husband. Michael was almost seven years old and Bernie was four. As she sat down with the children in the living room each one in a dilapidated easy chair, tears flowed from under her glasses. "I am very sad," she announced. "I would like you to behave well if only for a week. My daddy is gone."

David, was born on July 31, 1955. Marie came home on August 3rd, unable to rid herself of a nagging ache in her side. David was very sick with a high temperature. "Honey, what's the matter?"

Bermard would ask as tears filled Marie's eyes. "This is not normal pain," she replied.

The new pain would not subside, Marie was examined by several doctors throughout August. Most of them sent her home, but day by day the pain increased in intensity, and each doctor was unable to provide a diagnosis. Bernard and Marie took care of us and each other until the day that she could not get out of bed without collapsing--she looked like a puppet whose strings had been cut. The tears poured out of her. Her temperature rose and she was finding it difficult to breathe. Bernard's hair danced frantically around his fingers as he scratched his head. The writing in his journal stopped on August 10, Michael's birthday. "Nothing to celebrate," was all he could muster.

Chapter Six

"The ambulance screamed down our street, splashing the neighborhood houses with its red spinning light."

Ambulance

As the red ambulance light strobed our yellow house, I could see my mother in the bedroom. My father seemed desperate. He clenched his pipe tightly while attempting to help my mother to her feet, only to have her collapse in a heap. She sat on her bed, head down in front of her shaded window and we could only see her silhouette until Dad carried her out of the bedroom and placed her on the couch. The torrential flow of tears that had streamed down her cheeks subsided as she slipped into unconsciousness. When they took her out on the stretcher, I could see that her lips were blue. I noticed a trail of damp leaves had been tracked in by the ambulance men across the wooden floor, and I wondered if my mother would ever come home to sweep them. The whole neighborhood gathered around our home with gaping mouths, tears, and whispers. The ambulance screamed down our street, taking her away. Later that night when Dad returned, we were already in bed, but not sleeping. He wailed in his room, his voice echoing from down the hall like the futile cries from a distant torture chamber. All the while, his wife languished in the hospital, vacillating between the horror of reality and the unrelenting chaos of her dreams:

***

I am in an iron lung...Breath is important...It is a gift....It is from a machine...I speak...The machine grinds...I breathe...I speak...Nurses hover...Doctors poke...They open it up...They look at me...inside the iron lung.

The dreams are so vivid because of my fever. The dreams blend and flow. They let me walk and run. They fool me.

How are my children? Did I see my husband with the doctors talking or was that a dream? Michael is sick, I know he is but nothing is being done about it. How long has it been? I dream of a long train that whistles past and each car has ten windows. I am standing on the bank staring into each window passing by like frames of a movie. I dream that Michael is on the bed and like a limp rag every time I pick him up he drapes his arms over my shoulder. When I put him down on the bed he collapses.

There is screaming and darkness and there is a blinding light. In my dream frames of light pass by again. Dr. West speaks to me as the train screams by. It's his eyes behind the mask. If I could only know for certain that the children are O.K.

There are others...They breathe and dream...They yell and scream...The machines grind...We breathe...We speak...The machines grind...We think and dream...We are inside iron lungs.

More dreams are coming. The screeching train has become one of the more bearable ones. Neighbors yelling at me to get up and the children are vacant staring shells. Dinner is burning on the stove.

I am surfacing and the pitter of the nurses' voices surrounds me as I fight the light, the whiteness that keeps me under. "Marie, try to eat." The ward ripples as I probe the faces hovering over me. Briefly, I surface.

"I am not hungry...Michael is sick...Can't eat..."

Frames of light gush vertically and then flow horizontally. I am so dizzy. Each feverish frame melts into the next, windows passing until there is nothing but a glowing light.

On September 1, 1955, Marie Andree Mulligan was admitted to Chapin Hospital with polio. Although 90-95% of cases are similar to influenza, the polio virus has the ability to cause paralysis and even death. My mother contracted bulbospinal polio, the most severe form, affecting her ability to breathe, as well as causing complete paralysis from her neck down. Polio is transmitted through fecal matter and human contact. The local newspaper announced new cases every day. Ironically, a polio vaccine was available but free access was delayed by Congress. Our government viewed free medical care as the "back door to socialism."

The only solution for the many polio patients to stay alive was a massive, cage-like machine called an "iron lung". When a human inhales, the diaphragm and the muscles between the ribs contract which expands the chest cavity and draws in air. The muscles and the diaphragm then relax which makes the chest cavity smaller. This contraction pushes out the air that causes the body to exhale. An iron lung is a piece of equipment designed to facilitate the breathing of a person whose muscles have been paralyzed. It is a long steel cylinder large enough to fit a person. The patient's entire body is slid into the steel drum with the exception of their head. In order to instigate breathing the machine mechanically pumps air in and out of the cylinder. When pumped in, the air pressure exerted on the chest cavity is strong enough to force the body to exhale. When the air is pumped out, the lungs are freed to open back up to inhale.

Chapter Seven

"The realization that one can do nothing, not even raise one's head to defy the monotony, forces the mind to undertake the exhausting task of fantasy."

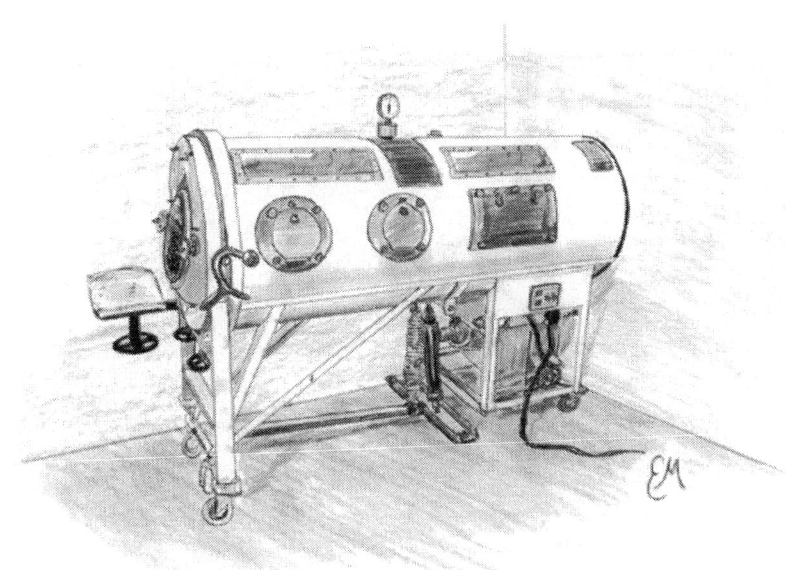

Iron Lung

In the hospital, Marie drifted in and out of consciousness for three weeks. She could not even breathe on her own. The iron lung that surrounded her cranked and churned while she dreamed of moving, only to wake up and suffer once again the horror of her paralysis. When her lucidity returned, Marie dissolved into a depression. Her senses were so acute that when the attendants washed her hair it was painful. Her nose itched and she could not scratch it. She could feel her toes when the sheets touched them but she could not respond with movement. Bernard pleaded with her to remain strong, to consider the children, and to believe that life had some good things left for her. Every night he sat next to her listening to her words of despair, only to return home to his four children and their needs. He wrote nothing at all in his journal--just one blank page after another, inscribing only the date, for three months.

At the ward, one day gave way to another, and the routine seemed to smother the enormity and shock of Marie's tragedy. Time was no longer measured in hours or days but by medications, treatments, and the appearance and disappearance of medical staff. In the hospital, time had no real meaning. Paralyzed, confined to a bed, surrounded by the bland colors of sheets and walls, she felt useless. She surrendered to the overwhelming tedium and its suffocating power. The realization that one can do nothing, not even raise one's head to defy the monotony, forces the mind to undertake the exhausting task of fantasy. It was novelty, not time, that marked the importance of the moment. Any event that pierced the ennui or that interrupted the dull parade of trivial occurrences seemed momentous. Visitors were so important, and yet so upsetting. She would notice the fidgeting, the glancing at the clock, and the pauses in conversation and invariably she felt the guilt of sharing her dreary existence with a loved one. At the end of the visit, as family and friends sauntered out to their busy lives, the drab walls would overpower her again and mock her belief that she belonged in the world outside the confines of the hospital.

Bernard's world of finding sitters, working, paying bills, and explaining his wife's condition to incredulous friends and relatives in

England and in Meadville became a grind. He arranged for Meme to come and help. Somehow, he still played the organ at the church, but he performed his music aggressively. He displayed his humor, but it could be mean-spirited, such as giving names to the hospital staff like "wretch" or "beehive". One man was referred to as "Chromosome." Yet, he obviously was sensitive to our happiness, because he would bring home little toys for Michael and me and put them beside the bed as a surprise for when we awoke. I remember getting all seven dwarf figurines from the Snow White story one by one over the course of a month or so.

Meme paced the floor parallel to the front door. This was the second day of her trip, and she was preparing to see Marie for the first time since her illness. She arrived in part to comfort her daughter, and also to placate the state social worker, who was concerned about our lack of supervision. We had been roving the neighborhood, daring other children to play "blood brothers", and parents complained. Meme's first responses to our community were unambiguous; she commented derisively on the dress, deportment, and general state of its blue-collar residents. Her remarks about America's "filthy streets and unkempt houses" were perhaps an outlet for her grief and frustration over her daughter's plight. Bernard tried to prepare her for the impending jolt of Marie's condition, and she nodded grimly. He opened the door for her as they left, and she stopped in the frame to look at him. In an unexpected outburst, she quietly scoffed, "tell your God when you pray that I despise him!" Her comment stung Bernard and he hung his head as he waited for her to exit. "We should get going," he muttered.

In the hospital corridor, Meme's pace quickened with the swing of Bernard's arm; he pointed out the iron lung that contained her daughter. She ran the last steps with her arms outstretched. Mother and daughter exploded into tears. They exclaimed and consoled one another in French, their shared language both a soothing gift and a substitute for privacy. Bernard watched from the threshold of the dividers, saddened even more deeply by the intensity of their moment. Meme's presence would lift Marie's spirits, he hoped.

Bernard and Marie knew that Meme would care for the children and would enrich our lives with loving care and lively conversation.

Chapter Eight - Despair

"I will do all in my power to make life satisfying for you."

St. Margaret's

Passing the nurse's station, a familiar feeling of sadness percolated within Bernard as Marie came into view, encapsulated by the iron lung. Other iron lungs were scattered down the ward, with privacy screens only a few feet apart to separate them. Bernard walked with purpose, but also with some trepidation. He had felt anxiety throughout the day, meditating on a group of poems that Marie had given to him. She had composed one poem, dictated to an orderly that Bernard found particularly disturbing:

The Snow fell softly in the night
With slow insistence covering
The moist earth, which yesterday
Was swelling with the warmth of spring.

The sunlit days passed early by,
The winter chill returned too soon
Clouding the fields, the trees, the sky.

Now there is so little left,
What is the use of questioning…
It may be there's greater plan
God may have need of suffering.

When composing poetry Marie formulated her ideas carefully, committing them to memory until she could speak to a scribe. The voice inside her head was contradicted by the unplanned and unwanted pauses imposed on her speech by the machine. She started writing in short stanzas so that she could physically complete a phrase. Although she had written all her life, her compositions were now more personally meaningful and prolific. Her writing effectively combated the monotony of each day, and filled her with a sense of capability through a means of expression. No improvement in her physical condition to be expected, thus, the arcs of her mind and the landscapes of her emotions were the most important for her to explore. Setting these adventures on paper was perhaps partially an act of defiance, a way to say, "I exist."

She did not anticipate the impact of her poem on her husband. Bernard was upset, and he showed the poem to Father Anthony at St. Margaret's Church one evening after Benediction. "I am very concerned about her," he reported. "She is on the verge of despair." Pushing the rims of his glasses up, Father Anthony considered the poem and its meaning. "Despair, as a predisposition to sin, would require a total abandonment of hope, as well as a cynical view of God's existence," the priest stated. Bernard found little comfort in Father Anthony's dry analysis. Her opportunity for eternal life in Heaven seemed assured by her suffering on Earth, he reasoned, but if she abandoned all hope even Heaven would be denied her. Sin or no sin, his wife's abandonment of hope chilled him to the core of his faith. As he pulled his chair alongside her head where it protruded from the iron lung, he kissed her. A tear dripped onto her face before he could catch it. "What's the matter, dear," she asked. "Your poem affected me," he answered softly. He placed the back of his hand gently on her cheek. "Do you still believe in God?" he asked. She turned her head away from his hand and looked in the opposite direction at a row of three iron lungs. As she turned back to him, her cheek touching his hand once again, she replied, "It's the Church, not God. I believe in God, but your faith is in the Catholic Church." She paused, choosing her words thoughtfully as she continued on. "No one from your Church or the Diocese has ventured into this little piece of Hell!"

His relief concerning her immortal soul was tempered by the anger that welled up within him. His faith, the faith he had insisted Marie convert to, had been tested by her struggle and had failed. He knew her assessment to be true; the Church had abandoned her. They gazed at one another quietly for the remainder of the visit, both so engaged in emotion that speech seemed inadequate. As he prepared to leave, Bernard glanced at his wife and he pondered his promise he made three years earlier, "I will do all in my power to make life satisfying for you." His power and his faith were being challenged.

His exhaustion left him vulnerable to the very despair he was asking his wife to denounce. As he drove home he resolved to confront the Church, and that night he wrote a letter to the Bishop to state his frustration.

Dear Bishop,

I have been living in Rhode Island for 5 years now and there are certain questions that I cannot find answers to. These questions bear on the differences between Catholicism as I once knew it and the Catholicism of Rhode Island. I am almost accustomed to paying fifteen cents at the door yet I shall never completely be resigned to PAYING my way into God's House as I do at the movies, concert or theater.

Another more serious difference is in the visitation of the sick by your clergy. As a child, I used to watch the Parish Priest and his curates plodding through all sorts of weather to the local hospitals both Catholic and City alike on their visits to the sick, not just Catholics. They attended to everyone who needed Hope!

Bernard Mulligan

Chapter Nine - David and Patrick

Patrick and David

During Marie's hospitalization, Patrick had been staying at the Cauley residence about a mile away. Gladys Cauley had volunteered to watch Patrick because of our difficulties. Still, Mrs. Cauley had her own troubles. Her husband stayed out often, and offered little assistance in looking after their children. In time, Patrick's stay there became permanent, and Bernard and Gladys became close. His charm and playful teasing, coupled with Gladys's encouragement and concern, set the foundation for a strong friendship. Bernard chose not to discuss his despair and loneliness with Marie, because her life had grown so wretched and full of depression. Thus, Gladys's willingness to allow my him to vent his feelings and frustration, as well as her availability to watch any of us at any time rendered her an indispensable resource. He was affectionate with Gladys in small ways. She would touch his hand as he talked at her kitchen table, and when she stood in front of the stove, he would cup his hand on her shoulder, to connect and make eye contact. Bernard would make her laugh and she would swat him gently on the arm. Gladys fortified my father against the brutal reality of two jobs, four children, and his true love's horrific condition. The intimacy between Bernard and Gladys might not have constituted an affair, but their bond was a threat to his marriage. When Marie came home, she demanded Patrick's return. She also insisted that Bernard end his relationship with Gladys. He was saddened, and his grudging compliance to his Marie's wishes combined with my mother's resentment towards Gladys remained a quiet issue throughout their lives.

Marie could see visitors approaching from the distant hall past the nurses' station. Her husband emerged from the dark corridor into the light as he walked methodically towards her. As always, he first stooped to kiss her, and then snapped the clipboard smartly off the side of the iron lung. He perused the vital signs and the doctor's scribbled morning notes. "What is the weather outside?" she asked. "It's strange," he replied casually. "There's a lot of fast moving grey clouds and the wind is kicking up the sand left by the snow removal trucks." He pulled a stool beside the iron lung and sat close to her face. She tilted her head to meet his gaze. He would eventually bring the stool to her other side, so that she could evenly use her neck. When she was very tired, he would simply place the stool at the front of the machine so that they could converse in the mirror above her head. "How is Patrick?" she asked. "Well, Gladys brought him by for trick or treat. Michael and Bernie were both distracted, and didn't seem to recognize or acknowledge him. Michael was getting into his altar boy vestments in preparation for Benediction and Bernie was developing his character for Halloween; he blackened his face with permanent marker—his face had to be cleaned with alcohol when he returned." Bernard loved to embellish stories from home to make her smile. However, David was in a cast after his recent operation and this was a serious matter. During his initial prognosis with polio, the doctors said that David would need a brace to walk in the future. Nonetheless, Bernard had read in a medical journal about an operation that could secure his paralyzed ankle so that a brace would not be needed. The procedure required the extraction of a piece of shin-bone for insertion into the ankle, like a splint. "David is giving Meme fits," he reported to Marie. "He screams and yells about the cast and his lack of mobility. He is pretty resentful of the rest of us walking around him. I asked Bernie to spend some time with him, but I got the 'do I have to?' routine."

Appointments with doctors, physical therapists, and x-ray technicians filled David's life as a child. At the end of the day, he spent most of his time in a chair or in bed, alone, and surrounded by toys and crayons. He would rarely answer when his name was called; he seemed lost in his quiet activities. Yet, we all attended to his needs as necessary, and he began to assume that they should be our priorities. In kindergarten, he was surprised that the teacher would not comply with his requests. Instead of following instructions at school, he passed in papers with lines and circles drawn haphazardly outside the borders of the page.

David dominated Meme's time, and if we became troublesome my father would be the one to hear about it as he came in the door from work. Before leaving to visit our mother, he would discipline us. We would try to plead our case during dinner, but he would just stare at us, his green eyes exhausted and menacing. "I'm eating!" he'd bark, "Do what Meme asks, whether you agree or not!"

David crawled until he was three years old. Sometimes Dad would pick David up and walk him around the house. He would approach the stairs and suddenly burst up the steps in a run, making David laugh. As he descended the stairs, he would feign extreme caution. "I hope we don't fall," he'd quiver. He'd then pretend to be fearful as he loosened his grip on his son to add to the drama. When he placed David back in his crib, the crying would start and Meme would come to the rescue as my father slipped out the side door. Dad could only play in brief spurts.

Chapter Ten - Chapin Hospital

Bunkers

Bernard fought with the staff at the hospital constantly, to provide Marie with even minimal care. As new cases arrived and the din of wheezing iron lungs increased, the personal care only deteriorated. It became apparent that if her teeth were to be brushed, that he would have to do it. The ward was crowded with adults and children in iron lungs, and the overworked and underpaid nurses struggled to meet the challenge. Of all the things that she was subjected to during her hospitalization, the most traumatic was her physical therapy treatment. She was lowered into a swimming pool by being placed in a canvas hammock suspended by an overhanging apparatus and slowly submerged up to her neck into the water. In Bernard's letters to his mother, he explained the phobia that Marie had developed and asked his mother to imagine the inability to move in water, one of the most automatic responses in human nature. Marie's fear of drowning was intertwined with the reality of her paralysis. Over time, she began to have a recurring dream about being afloat in an iron lung in the ocean. When she would awake from her dream, she would often be in tears, terrified. She would go on to describe this experience to others for many years

In January of 1956, complaints about Chapin hospital resulted in a formal investigation of the quality of care. Marie and Bernard received a questionnaire from the committee. Despite their experience, they answered the questions politely. The finalized report focused on the issue of substandard nursing care. Inadvertent torture best describes the effect of poor care on a paralyzed patient, for whom there is no consolation in waiting. When Bernard would arrive, he would be disgusted when he found that the iron lung was a mess, and that Marie had not seen a nurse or attendant all day. Perhaps, her despondency allowed Marie to be oblivious to the miserable conditions, but it did not offer Bernard any solace. The wife he loved was paralyzed, dissociated, and miserable. It would infuriate him when the staff would talk about her at her bedside as if she were unable to hear or understand. Once, and only once, a nurse referred to her as "the poor thing." My father went into a rage, and although I have no recollection of what he said, I remember that we could hear his yelling from our position at the open window. It frightened me to hear his voice at that volume.

Bernard's disdain for doctors who became hospital administrators took root during the time of Marie's convalescence. Chapin Hospital's chief administrator at the time was Dr. Connor, who became concerned about the proliferation of food and candies being brought in by patients, relatives, and friends. To Dr. Connor, this was appalling and by the authority of his position, ceased this practice by decree. Bernard refuted this policy by letter, and his restrained eloquence did little to obscure his anger and disbelief. He wrote:

Dear Doctor Connor,

I wish to protest your recent order forbidding outside food or candy for patients in the West I Ward. I do this from interest in the welfare of these patients and with some understanding of the problems which prompt you to take such action. The reasons for my protests are these:

These patients are really people, human beings, and not merely polios or respirators. The pleasures of life are fantastically restrained for them. The pleasure of eating is one of the few left to them. No one can well argue that any institutional food is adequate in this respect. This interdict removes an important feature of their present life and, therefore, can have a greater or lesser effect on the psychological and physical effect depending on the person involved. This action is negative in another way. It robs the relatives of the sadly small satisfaction of being some use to their loved ones. It also actually militates against the physical welfare of the patient by depriving them of wholesome food attractive to their personalized palate. In this connection, I wish to state categorically that Mrs. Mulligan has always received dietetically satisfactory food from myself and her mother, Mrs. A. Cooper. In this matter, we consulted Dr. Medina and followed scrupulously his advice. The interim of time between supper and breakfast is too long, and it is common knowledge that a prolonged fast can destroy appetite as well as whet it in people so drastically reduced in physical activity. A general rule of this sort, while aiming at abuses, is merely running away from the responsibility of discussing abuses with the particular individuals guilty of them.

Sincerely,
Bernard J. Mulligan

Although he railed against the administration of the hospital for its absurd policies, his greatest challenge was to get the best physical care for Marie. There were few treatments for the chronic and incurable paralysis resulting from polio. Hot packs, massage, and muscle manipulation were prescribed. Patients who could not breathe without the iron lung were taught how to swallow air. Polio patients needed to learn this skill to help them survive power outages. Every day in Bernard's diaries, he noted the length of time that Marie could breathe outside the iron lung. She could only last 7-12 minutes at first, and her release from the hospital depended on the improvement of this ability. After a year she was able to last 25-30 minutes.

The smallest head cold could be catastrophic to polio patients. The contraction of pneumonia ensured death, and nurses and doctors always wore masks to prevent the spread of germs. Eventually, we were allowed to visit, but prior to that, we could only see her through a window. A mirror was placed on an angle above her head where it protruded out of the iron lung. Subsequently, we merely saw each other's reflection. Her sentences were short when she spoke, because the words were arranged around the mechanical work of the iron lung. Every few seconds the iron lung would force its will on her breathing. One could speed it up or slow it down, but the patient's conversation had to give in to the timing of the iron lung.

"How was school..........today, Bernie?"

Pictures of Michael, Patrick, David, and myself were scotch-taped next to the mirror on the iron lung. After arriving at the hospital and visiting with my mother, Michael and I would conduct our war games on the hospital grounds. My father would go back into the hospital and we'd run out to the grassy yard, carrying our plastic weapons. There were cement enclosures around every basement window and these became our bunkers. Michael was always the

American and I was the enemy. The enemy was usually Japanese, Mexican, or German. My role was to be the dying enemy soldier, clutching my heart and falling to the ground.

Bernie and Michael, Chapin Hospital

Chapin Hospital became something of a community. There was a hospital newspaper, and Marie wrote articles for it. The articles in the hospital newspaper announced birthdays and patients' visits home, or shut-in parties. Shut-in parties would combine people with other afflictions like Multiple Sclerosis and Lou Gehrig's disease with the polio patients, and assemble them all with their loved ones. The afflicted would arrive in vans and ambulances with their families at a designated cafeteria. The food would come, and husbands would feed wives and wives would feed husbands. I looked around in amazement as kindness mingled with chaos. The ever-still polio patients juxtaposed with the spasms of Multiple Sclerosis patients. Michael sulked unhappily, uncomfortable with our newly imposed celebrity, while my father's jaw remained locked in a smile. His meal went uneaten as the mashed potatoes, peas, and tough meat were usually cold, and the general disorder was upsetting.

The hospital would come to life during visitors' hours. Husbands and wives could stay longer than friends and clergy. Tears would flow when someone would leave abruptly, unable to cope with the sight of their wretched loved one. Absolute despair reigned when a spouse no longer came to visit. After the first year and a half of my mother's hospitalization, we were allowed into the polio ward and from time to time my father would send us off to see patients with no visitors.

Part Two

Weary Child

Lately, I get the impression
That; thoughts worn by a smile
Frail and idly listing
Make a weary child.

Chapter Eleven - A New Life

Home for Christmas, Mrs. Bernard Mulligan is surrounded by her family, Bernard Jr. (left), 7; Patrick, 3; Mrs. Andree Cooper (her mother), Mr. Mulligan holding David, 2; and Michael, 9, opening one of the first gifts.
—State Staff Photo by William F. Geerhold

Mulligans Get Wonderful Yuletide—Mommy's Home

Providence Journal, 1958

Months and years passed and the hospital ward changed. It was less crowded as a result of deaths or patients' return to their homes. No one was cured. Some unfortunate patients were placed in sanitariums. The question for each patient became: is life worth living and, if so, how would one survive? The question of happiness was too complex for consideration. Bernard and Marie's singular purpose in life became preparation for an eventual return to her home and integration into the world she had lost. My mother would come home for weekends, at first, as a trial. The ambulance would arrive and she would be wheeled in through the front door. At the end of her visit the ambulance would return and she'd be wheeled out again, usually in tears. Hospital life had become routine and a little brighter, but all my mother could think of was Ruth Avenue. To prepare for home life polio patients were fitted with a portable lung. This was comprised of a turtle shell type of device that was placed on the upper body, and a hose that was connected to the middle of the shell. Air would be forced into the shell to manipulate the lungs. The portable lung was connected to a battery or plugged into a wall socket. If a patient was to go home, either an iron lung or a rocking bed would have to be installed in the house. A rocking bed operated like a metronome or a see-saw. The head of the bed would raise and then lower. As the head rose, the patient's lungs opened, and when it declined, the lungs would close. It had an electric motor, a fan belt, and a crank assembly.

A rocking bed was wheeled into our home. Mirrors were placed strategically so that her view could be expanded to other rooms. I wasn't prepared for what I saw when she arrived. Polio patients' bodies shrink in response to the atrophy of muscles, so my mother's head seemed enormous when I first saw her in a wheelchair. Her hands were cupped over the ends of the armrests. A flower was taped to the rising and falling chest-piece. We all gathered around her touching her hands. As they pulled her up the stairs in through the front door, she looked all around the living room. Newspaper reporters met her for the story; her smile was a bit weary throughout their probing. After they left, she asked to be wheeled by the living room window. As she gazed out at the flashing Christmas lights, she began to hope that there might be life after polio.

Patrick and David brought her pictures and climbed on her wheelchair. They did not seem to notice or care that our mother was so different from the other mothers in the neighborhood. Meme had cared for them all of their lives but now it would be under the auspices of my mother, planned secretly in French. Patrick was four, David was three. They accepted life as it was, not questioning, not complaining.

Michael and I lay on our army cots the night she came home, staring at the unfinished ceiling and ruminating about the return of our mother, he said to me, "I hate it when people stare." "Me too!" I replied.

That winter blurred quickly into spring, not only because we were young, but because each day was thoroughly busy. Our new lives required unique routines. The sheer pace of chores, schoolwork, playtime, church, and neighborhood company allowed us to adjust quickly from any sadness or anxiety our mother's paralysis had brought. Bernard modeled perserverance, and Marie projected hope as best she could.

***

"Mulligan's residence!" Bernard's voice rang out almost defiantly. He was standing by the window, staring out, as the telephone cord vibrated down each tight spiral. He gripped the phone and listened, his face twitching as if he were working through a puzzle. "Well, I am sure Marie will be thrilled," he said as he broke into a smile. "What does it mean, though?" I always watched him closely. There was never anything contrived or affected about my father. On the contrary, he often seemed to be purely reactive. Suddenly, he knocked on the window to get the attention of someone in the front yard. He pointed to his own two eyes first and then to an assumed perpetrator, mouthing the words, "I'm watching you."

"We could certainly use the cash," he answered. "We would do just about anything to show our appreciation to the March of Dimes. I don't know what we would do without you." He was listening. Taking off his glasses, Bernard rubbed his eyes. "Sure, sure... of course, no doubt... absolutely. I can't wait." He eased the phone gently on the receiver. As he turned to walk into Marie's room, he caught me eavesdropping. "We are going to do some solicitation, Bernie. Your mother is Polio Mother of The Year, 1958." Was it a grimace or a smile on his face? One never knew.

I ran outside to tell Michael, who was probably the guilty party that my father was watching. Michael had a jack knife that he had taken up throwing into the turf of the yard. He had an assortment of younger children gasping and clucking at his brazen, precise knife work, narrowly missing his own foot each time. "Michael, Michael," I yelled. "We are going to do some solicitation with Ma in the parking lot of the A&P. Dad wants us to wear our baseball uniforms." Michael pulled the knife out of the ground, wiped the blade on his jeans, and folded it shut. "Great," he muttered sarcastically as he slid the jack-knife into the front pocket of his jeans.

On Saturday, Dad pulled into the A&P parking lot, and parked near the entrance of the store. He retrieved the wheelchair from the trunk and opened the front passenger door. Michael climbed into the front seat and unplugged Marie from the chest-piece. He and my father picked my mother up and gently deposited her into the wheelchair. I plugged her hose back in. A card table was set up with a donation sign-up sheet. Michael and I positioned ourselves on either side of my mother. My father drove off to play the organ at the church. Store customers would smile warmly as they walked up to us. They each wrote their telephone number, address, and donation promise on the ledger. "Thank you," Marie would say as she proudly displayed her *1958 Polio Mother of The Year* button that rose up and down on her breathing apparatus. As the day progressed, the store customers dwindled. The three of us stared quietly at the parking lot as we sat under the shade of the awning. A man approached us. He wore a janitor's outfit with a jumble of keys on his belt that jingled as he strode purposely to the table. He signed the ledger and before my mother could say her line, he looked at me and asked a familiar question, "Can she talk?" I looked at Michael and queried, "Can she talk?" Michael glanced down at our mother. "I dunno, can you talk?" "No, not really," my mother replied. Michael looked at me and answered. "No, she can't." "No she can't," I replied to the man. "That's too bad," sighed the janitor who was oblivious to our well-rehearsed prank.

The man entered the store and disappeared from view. Michael shook his head. "What an idiot!" he derided. "Now, now," Marie cautioned. "Be kind."

Chapter Twelve - Routine

Bernard at the Piano

1958 was a difficult year everywhere in America, but especially in our home. The US was in the deepest financial recession since World War II, and unemployment soared. Yet paradoxically, around our house on Ruth Avenue, growth was everywhere. The elm trees that lined the street were beginning to uproot and crumble the sidewalks, the few lawns that existed were well-trampled, and because no one owned a garage, cars were parked haphazardly on the street. Children were so ubiquitous that cars driving down the street would have to wait for the herd of kids to move before progressing. Fortunately, the paranoia about Polio had subsided as the cases disappeared, and life moved on. Each of our neighbors even signed a note expressing their sympathy for our situation, and donated a dollar each to help cover expenses. Their kindness paid for one month's rent.

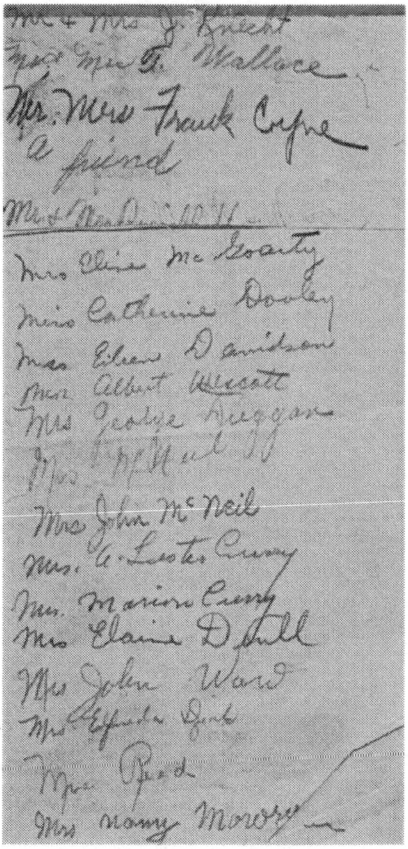
Mr & Mrs J. [illegible]
Mr & Mrs T. Wallace
Mr & Mrs Frank Cope
a friend
Mr & Mrs [illegible]
Mrs Olive McGoarty
Miss Catherine Dooley
Mrs Eileen Davidson
Mrs Albert Wescott
Mrs George Duggan
Mrs [illegible]
Mrs John McNeil
Mrs G. Lester Curry
Mrs Marion Curry
Mrs Elaine D [illegible]
Mrs John Ward
Mrs [illegible]
Mrs Reed
Mrs Nancy Morrow

Life settled into a routine of shopping for food, feeding the Siamese cats, cooking, ironing, and playing. My mother insisted on doing our homework with us. Michael helped with my mother's written correspondence to friends and businesses as did the women who came in to care for Mom during the day when my father was at work. Remarkably, at ten years of age, Michael was more literate than most of the help and his handwriting more clear and precise. The March of Dimes paid families $100.00 a week for nursing assistance. My parents paid the aides $50.00 a week, and spent the other $50.00

on miscellaneous needs. As our new life required constant adaptation, Dad invented a mouth-stick that my mother could use to turn pages in her books, which were held on a stand resembling a music sheet holder on a piano. She had a cup holder also, and my father made long, bent glass straws in his lab at work so that she could have her tea, coffee, or scotch. As my father fed her, he would discuss his day at work and she would talk about her day at home.

Michael and I did a lot of housework to pitch in, and my father insisted on giving us an allowance. Payday would be on Friday, but the amount tendered would be commensurate with the quality of the work done. On one occasion I vacuumed upstairs, but was docked on payday; my mother said that although the vacuum cleaner was obviously running, it did not move, and she deduced that I was reading comics.

The mirrors around the house gave my mother a view into most of the rooms on the first floor. A tilted mirror on the front door gave her a view up the stairs. All cupboards were numbered and all bookcases were lettered; she knew exactly where all the groceries were, as well as all the books, cooking appliances, and records. My mother was like a mainframe computer server, compiling the information in her brain as she sat up in her bed, controlling every aspect of the household. When the groceries came in from the car they would be placed on the kitchen table, and one by one each item was held up to her reflection in the mirror for instructions. "Cupboard seven, middle shelf behind the baked beans," she'd say.

Every day the mailman, the laundry man, the milkman, and the vegetable man would come and conduct business with her. Over time, they would come to have coffee, and my mother would extract the details of their lives and jobs. She would advise them, or help them with writing a letter to their boss, or remind them to get flowers for their wives. Once she told the vegetable man that he would be better received by the neighbors if he bathed more often. We were all glad that he took her advice. The cats also quickly figured out who was boss. They'd jump in her lap, rub their faces on her chest-piece, and in no time at all, she would find a volunteer: "Bernie, would you feed the cats?"

An ambulance would arrive occasionally to take my mother back to the hospital whenever she got a bad cold. The decision to have her return to the hospital had become increasingly disruptive and unpleasant for everyone, because she had become an integral part of the workings of the house and the flashing lights and commotion raised the collective anxiety level. If she wasn't at home, the cats, the mailman, the laundryman, and the vegetable man would all mope and meander as if their world had suddenly gone black and white. Without a central point of authority, my brothers and I floundered. One gets used to the idea of having someone to tell you what to do. Having surrendered the decision-making process to my mother, we were suddenly vulnerable to chaos if she left. The house now occupied by six cats, four children, my father, and anywhere from ten to twenty white mice in the basement. Beyond that, the house was visited daily by neighbors, the attending nurse, and the vendors. Door-to-door salesmen roamed the streets of our neighborhood, selling all sorts of appliances and supplies. My mother talked to all of them. When she came back from the hospital, usually after a week or two, regulation and order would return, chores would get done, and life would become what we perceived to be normal. With only one bathroom, my mother would even decide whose turn it was to shower in the morning. A timer was set to ensure that the schedule would be maintained and that we would get to school on time, each of us carrying a paper bag with our name on it, containing a sandwich and a cookie.

The cats were an important part of the household. Mickey was the father Siamese cat, Penny was the mother, and they had three grown offspring together, named Moe, Larry, and Curly. Lucky, the sixth cat, was only part Siamese, but Penny still cared for her when she had come along as the lone survivor of a stray's litter. We all loved the cats even though my father was allergic. The cats co-existed with the mice that my father had for study in the basement. He had a mouse named Mittens that he decided would become a pet, and he gave him a cage of his own, separate from the others. One of our chores was to clean the mouse cages. During one of my mother's absences, I was cleaning Mitten's cage and Larry suddenly appeared--he grabbed Mittens and critically injured the poor mouse before I could save him. Dad did not blame me. He knew that things like this could happen with my mother gone. When my mother returned, a procedure was put into place that required the closing of the basement door and the evacuation of all cats present prior to opening the cage of a mouse. She reminded us of the procedure every time the cages were to be cleaned.

Of all the policies and procedures that were established and implemented, the governance of smoking constituted the most frequently revised and reviled institution. My father smoked a pipe, the aroma of which had to be controlled, but inexplicably, my mother decided that she wanted to smoke cigarettes. Initially, someone would stand in front of her having lit the cigarette and drawn it once or twice, bring it to my mother's lips so that she could inhale. Smoke would drift up her face like a transparent, rising curtain, and it was remarkable that any of the nicotine-filled smoke entered her lungs at all. It was a ritual that comforted her, adding to the limited amount of stimulation one deprived by paralysis could derive. Eventually, a device, which consisted of a copper shell sewn into a beanbag with a cigarette holder fastened to it, was developed. The smoking procedure changed with this invention; after initiating the process by starting a cigarette, one would simply put the beanbag device on my mother's chest-piece as it ascended and descended, install the fuming cigarette in the holder, and walk away. My mother would draw on it at her leisure. To see her drink scotch and smoke a cigarette at the same time, witnessing the concentration and flexing of her facial muscles, was like observing a trapeze artist. She would draw on the glass straw first, and having pulled the desired liquid, she'd gulp, and with the straw captured in the corner of her mouth, she would then swivel and draw on the cigarette. As the veil of smoke drifted up her face she would then relax, gaze out the window, and savor the interaction of alcohol and nicotine.

One day as I walked home from school, I noticed a commotion

in the distance near our house. As I focused on the scene, I observed the familiar blinking of an ambulance light. I was confused because my mother didn't have a cold that morning before I left for St. Margaret's school. I ran as fast as I could and cut through the growing crowd to see my mother, on a stretcher, being slid in through the back door of the ambulance with her arm bandaged, and tears rolling down her face. I searched for Michael in the crowd, my heart racing to find out what was going on. When I found him, he told me that our mother was enjoying scotch and a smoke when the cigarette holder fell off the chest-piece and landed on her arm. She screamed in agony, each cry contorted by the respirator, until someone arrived to get the burning cigarette off her arm. The burn was severe, and she was hospitalized for a week. She quit smoking, the bean-bag holder was thrown away, and intercoms were installed throughout the house. The intercom would be turned on if my mother was going to be alone.

The intercom installation rendered my mother omnipresent in the house, at least, in terms of sound. The house was absolutely alive 24 hours a day. At night, the rocking bed with its hum of a motor and the rhythmic squeaking of the floor, combined with the nocturnal activities of the cats, the snoring from my dad and the scurrying of mice in their cages, blended like the sound of an amateur jug band. After the addition of the intercom, my mother's bed was amplified in the speakers and imbued with high frequency from the little receiver, throughout the rooms, adding to the strange music of our home.

However, it was only the sound of her voice that would wake us up. "Bernard?" she would whisper as if trying to find him somewhere off in the dark. Michael and I would always wake up, but if my father had too much to drink the night before, or if he was exhausted or sick, he would not. Since I shared my father's name, I always woke up when she whispered. Michael or I could usually deal with her issue, unless it was a bedpan, and before too long I learned that skill. Luckily, she slept well and had a strong bladder, so most nights we all slept until dawn.

Every morning, 45 minutes were spent on getting my mother ready for the day, as she needed many adjustments in the positioning of pillows and of her torso. My father showed us how to move her leg up and down as we spoke to her, and set up her "hip pad" where most of the weight of her body met the bed. A telephone was set up next to her bed by Mr. McNulty, our next door neighbor who worked for the phone company, and it had a head-set that we would put on her head before dialing a number. This phone had major implications in our lives. For example, my mother could now call the school, the headquarters of The March of Dimes, and The Hitching Post Bar. Her access to the telephone led to occasional incidents of coerced self-incrimination. Michael got in trouble from time to time for mouthing off to one of the women who cared for my mother. He would immediately be ushered into our mother's room, the doors would be closed, and he would be asked to put the head-phone on her head and then he would dial Dad's office. Once my father was reached, Michael would be told to go to the other phone to be reprimanded. Glumly, he would say hello and listen as Bernard received the report. "Wait until I get home, young man!" was the standard response. Michael would take the head set off Marie's head, and go in his room to stew in trepidation. Sometimes, Dad would forget and our mother would not want to intrude into his schedule to remind him of the crime committed earlier. On these occasions, my mother would often say, "Let's keep this our little secret," changing her role as principal accuser to become an accomplice or confidant. As children, we alone understood the perversity of being asked to carry out one's own execution, and then to be saved by the architect of our demise.

It was difficult for my father to arrange for a doctor to make a house-call, if my mother was feeling ill. We would drive her to the doctor's office in the Buick and wait in the parking lot or bring her into the office on a stretcher. Michael and I could handle one end and my father could handle the other, and we'd parade her through the waiting room, followed by her breathing apparatus, into the treatment room. My Dad would stay with her while we were excused to the waiting room. My father's feeling about doctors, formed by these experiences and by his work at the Veteran's Administration, was not particularly kind. In his diary, on September 15th, 1961, he wrote about his sentiments under the title:

My Thanks to the Medical Profession

Thanks to Doctor West for not using domes on tanks, for not providing physical therapy, for his defeatist philosophy. To Doctor Dillan for wild rides to the hospital, for lack of courage, for HIS defeatist attitude, for recommending Marie be incarcerated in a hospital. To Doctor Joyce for two days in delaying Marie's polio diagnosis, for his ignorance of respiratory problems and equipment, for not wanting to see Marie because 'he'd been up since 5:30 AM!' To Doctor Alton Powell for his arrogance combined with ignorance, for his avarice, in fact, thanks for nothing. Thanks to the whole medical profession for their brain-washed members. Thanks to Dr. Hoffman for his sincere lack of interest.

My father's grueling schedule and the tacit expectation that he would solve all of our family's unsual and frequently perilous problems engendered righteous anger within him. It seemed as if most doctors forgot their duty to treat a human being and not merely a chart when they were confronted with the hardship of polio. Though his faith had always led him to believe that miracles were possible, it is unlikely that he ever anticipated manifesting them himself. Our mother, despite her condition, tried to utilize her cleverness to work out a routine in which she could be helpful; but there was no denying that the formula ultimately depended on Dad.

Chapter Thirteen

"Soon the chaos that existed in our home became a road show..."

1955 Buick Special

My father purchased a 1955 Buick Special in 1958, and it was decided that we could fit the portable respirator in the backseat and my mother could ride shotgun. My mother wanted to see the ocean. "It is always exhilarating to visit the sea," she exclaimed. Our favorite beach destination was Lido's Beach, where a large green expanse of crab grass served as a parking lot. The owners were forewarned of our arrival, and promised us that a space would be available up front, where the grass met the sand. She would be able to watch the waves and the people, and smell the ocean. My father took a weekday off from work to avoid the crowds. We traveled down Ruth Avenue towards the Red Bridge that crossed the Providence River to the East Side. Route 95 did not exist; if one were to drive to the beach, one would take Route 1 or 1A through Providence, Cranston, Warwick, East Greenwich, Wakefield, North and South Kingston, and finally into the Narragansett beach area. It soon became apparent on our trip that the seat belt and pillows we had strategically placed around my mother did not prevent her from falling sideways--so my brother Michael and I took turns holding her. She marveled at the experience. She commented on how green everything seemed, but she was particularly moved by the clouds and wind. She had become an acute observer of the world. Although it was a long hour drive of traffic lights and congestion, she absorbed every minute, quietly entranced.

Once we arrived at the beach, my brother Michael and I headed straight into the waves, while our mother and father sat in the car with the windows open and the radio playing classical music. The steady, rhythmic slapping of the waves, the warmth of the morning sun, and the smell of the salty air were all such a contrast to the hospital atmosphere that she had endured for the past three years. Michael and I rode the waves for hours, coming out of the water only for lunch. The battery of my mother's respirator began running low, and we started home just after finishing our hot dogs.

During the ride home, as I held my mother's shoulders, I fell asleep. My father stopped short at a red light and my mother pitched forward out of my arms, pulling the hose out of her chest-piece. She was in pain as we straightened her up and plugged the hose back in. Nothing was said for the rest of the ride, as Michael took over the duty of holding her in place and I skulked in shame in the back seat. Despite the difficulties of keeping her upright and the cramped conditions in the car, the trip was the most liberating experience that Marie had since her paralysis. Our father remembered his promise to make life satisfying for her, and constantly schemed to improve upon her limited opportunities for stimulation.

Dad with 1948 Reo Bus

On August 5th, 1960, a curious article appeared in the Providence Journal. It was very short, but it included a picture of a man and wife surrounded by nine children, sitting on and around the snout of a school bus. John Caffrey lived in Albuquerque, New Mexico, and he had purchased a school bus for $100. He fixed it up, and he and his family drove six days to Westfield, New Jersey, where his brother lived. My father read this article while drinking tea in his lab at the Veteran's Administration. Leaning back in his office chair he closed his eyes and pondered the logistics he would face if he converted a bus to meet Marie's challenges. He decided that he should buy a bus, install a rocking bed, and attach a generator in the back. Nine months later, after negotiating a second rocking bed from the March of Dimes, getting up the courage to ask for financial assistance from Meme, and subsequently, buying a generator, a 1948 Reo Bus was procured. It was May 9th, 1961. The bus had no seats or wheels when my father looked it over. Yet, when he put the key in the ignition, it started, and the salesman, Mr. Ripa, "seemed very sincere and honest." He purchased it for $200.00; North Scituate Motors towed it to our house and deposited it on the street with only three tires. After buying two new tires and tubes for $108.11, my father purchased plywood for the floor and $10.00 worth of paint for the interior. He started his first of many Bus Logs, and in it my father had sketches of the floor of the bus that he used to configure the rocking bed and bunk beds. He also saved receipts and made notes on gasoline purchases. Within a day or two, the beds were installed and the interior was painted. We made local trips during this construction phase. A steel platform was welded outside the emergency door in the back of the bus and the generator was bolted on the plate. On the trial run, it only took a few minutes to vibrate the bolts loose, and the generator tumbled onto the pavement. If a source of portable electric power was not available to my mother, then only short trips were possible, making the work of installing a generator critical. Many men in the neighborhood lent their expertise and opinions, as well as the spare parts that dwelled in their basements. The approach to the construction of the bus was to use the components available and make them work. The bolts that were designed into the platform were not standard, so the replacements one could find were usually a slightly different thread size.

The first trip with my mother was to the little league field where Michael played for the Rumford Lions and I played for Fram. Fram manufactured air and oil filters in our town and was a great sponsor. On the way to the baseball field, my father kept looking at my feet. Ked's sneakers had a large rubber piece located over the toes, and it was customary for boys to write their names or decorate this part of their apparel. Some older children would write obscenities or other words that would constitute a breach of conformity. I had chosen to write the same word on both of the toes of my sneakers. Of course, I knew that my father would see the word and would be disappointed or angry, but he only looked puzzled. I had written "FOT"; I thought I was so daring, and I was ready to suffer the consequences of my eight year old venture into the language of bodily functions. "I give up!" my father said. "What are you trying to say?" I could not believe his incomprehension, but I also had not looked up the word in the dictionary. As he drove, his pipe shifting, I could see his brain grappling with the letters and soon he stopped the bus. "Do you mean 'fart', because if that's what you mean, you're wrong." My Rhode Island accent had betrayed me, and I had simply spelled the word the way it was pronounced. Both my father and mother laughed all the way to the baseball field, and I was embarrassed of my exposed ignorance.

After the game, we drove the bus to the grocery store before heading home, but once we tried to leave the store parking lot the bus stalled. Police and Fire vehicles came to accompany us as we were towed back home. Everywhere we went we were a spectacle, my mother beaming from the bed with a chest-piece and hose and my father at the steering wheel with his pipe. As if to render the bus more conspicuous, the top was painted bluebonnet and the lower half was painted silver. The children in our neighborhood joined in the fun, because a bus with no seats was very close to a circus ride. Soon the chaos that existed in our home became a road show, as the bus was recognized while it traveled around the town. Meme returned to RI in time for a trip to Meadville, Pennsylvania, to visit the Mulligan Family. She was thrilled at the adventure, and happy for her daughter whose exuberance was contagious.

Some panels had been taken out of the roof and side of the bus and replaced by safety glass, in order to facilitate my mother's view on the world--its clouds, moon, and stars. The starvation for visual stimulation that she'd experienced during her exile in Chapin Hospital left her with a perpetual awe of the streams, ocean, and mountains, now wonderfully framed in the rectangular panorama of the new window. "Oh my," she'd whisper to herself if she viewed a storm cloud, or even just a big tree as she gazed out the bus window.

***

The crew did not leave until 2 PM, as the preparations prior to departure dragged on. The most daunting task was the installation of an outdoor generator. My mother was not going to take any chances; her attention to detail became an anchor. She inspected all of our duffel bags and the cooler for preparedness. My father attended to the bus arrangements. On board were: Mom, Dad, Meme, our cousin Joe Patrick, Michael, myself, Patrick, and David. The odometer was at 39,936 miles and the generator roared endlessly in the background. My father described the first day in his log:

Trip to Meadville, Pennsylvania August 1st, 1961

"Troubles began quickly--the generator vibrated loose shortly before Uxbridge, Massachusetts, and luckily was still running as it lay in the road. It sustained considerable damage to the muffler, but we got it bolted on again and managed to get going making such a racket that we couldn't hear the bus motor. We stopped fruitlessly trying to get bolts for the muffler. No soap! Marie's battery was running down steadily. Shortly after stopping at the fair, the motor started to have fits. We limped into a gas station, had the oil cap cleaned and a lawn motor muffler was put on the generator. We stopped before Charlton on Route 20 when the generator acted up. It was loose. I tightened the bolts and it smoothed out. This was after we finally got what looked like a mechanic to fiddle around. We had supper at a diner near where we had stopped to tighten the generator. $5.00 gone easily. I started the motor, but it is missing a bit now so about 7 PM we pulled into the trailer park and plugged in for the night. ($4.00) Right now, momentous preparations for returning and removing a large share of the contents of the bus, putting up curtains, planning sleeping accommodations. David is perserveringly underfoot and vocal. Pat is a little better. 8:40 PM: Two little

ones and Bernie bedded down in their bunks with Joe Pat outside in a sleeping bag. Lord knows how long it will take for the varmints to go to sleep as they are talking and laughing together. Flosone has been dished out to David, Gastursin and Dorbane for Marie, antihistamines for Bernie and I am taking my narcotic and so is Meme and Marie. I killed two mosquitos, so far. Bernie was fussing over Michael's debt of $0.20, so in disgust I paid it off."

It took three days to get to Pittsfield. Mom and Meme and we five boys were having a great time, but Dad was wearing down. He had total responsibility and yet, very little authority; every decision required placating my mother and grandmother. The consequences of my mother's disappointment were immense for him, and as the family treasurer, Meme's approval loomed over him as well. In his log, a great fatigue is evident. He negotiated with trailer park and motel owners, convincing them that the circus-like bus and its troupe should be allowed to take over their business for the night. He fixed the generator, nursed the engine of the bus, cooked the hot dogs and beans, enforced my mother's decisions concerning sleeping arrangements, and attended to his wife's physical needs. Joe Patrick, our cousin, was 15. He became Dad's first sergeant, cajoling Michael and me into games of Monopoly or just playing catch. David and Patrick, at 4 and 5 years of age, were the responsibility of Meme, but everyone knew the general was the woman in the bed, peering through the plexiglass.

When we left Pittsfield, we stayed on Route 20, and at my mother's insistence we picked up a young couple hitch-hiking. As it turned out, they were French Canadian and heading up to Montreal. It didn't take long for the bus to explode into a heated discussion *en Français.* Meme, my mother, and the couple were animated in their conversation. My father was looking ahead, his pipe billowing smoke like a locomotive, and we were all mesmerized by the babble and commotion. As we approached Albany, the tone became more serious. Obviously, the young couple were telling a story and by the outpouring of sympathetic gestures coming from Meme and Mom, the story was a sad one. Soon, the conversation stopped and my mother beckoned my father, in English, to pull onto at the shoulder of the road. He was directed to her bedside, where she told him to take down their address and give them five dollars. Intense whispering ensued and it was clear that my father had an objection to this financial transaction. "They will pay us back next week," my mother stated. We dropped the couple off amidst great displays of gratitude and warm feelings. For many years, thereafter, my father would inquire, upon returning from work, as if the check was expected imminently: "Surely, the money has come?" My father's words were often met with an angry stare from my mother, and occasionally laughter.

The green hills of eastern upstate New York with its sprawling farms, shimmering creeks, and winding dirt roads drifted by the bus windows. In the back, my mother was wistfully staring and sighing at the scenery while my father was driving. With his pipe tightly clenched, he would climb up a hill at ten miles per hour and coast down the other side at fifty miles per hour. He often smiled in his side mirror as the growing line of cars inched along in our wake, the loud growl of the generator hurling abuse at the car directly behind it. Dad would only pull over once ten cars amassed, and then listen contently to the angry profanities and bleating horns from the passing travelers, probably late for work. He would wave to them, mouthing thank you's and love you's with a grin. Meme sat in the comfortable chair behind him, knitting and remarking at the scenery to my mother. Michael, Joe Patrick and I were in the back playing games, arguing, or listening to the transistor radio. Patrick and David usually sat on the bunk beds making unheeded demands or falling asleep. The first few days consisted of sleeping in tents, on the floor of a cabin, or just under the bus. We were all very tired. Just outside of Schenectady, my father pulled into the L&M Motel. Lou Martin, the owner, and his wife cheerfully came out to greet us. The woman had a flowered, sleeveless apron over a contrasting striped blouse, and Lou wore a janitorial shirt and pants with keys hanging from his belt. "Holy Mackerel!" she exclaimed cheerfully. "Where are you from and please tell me you are staying the night!" We had not received a welcome like this before--people usually viewed us with trepidation, at least initially. Meme looked at my mother and nodded; she replied, "Yes... I guess we are." We all came running from the back of the bus to look out the window at an almond-shaped, blue bottomed pool with a diving board. The pool was surrounded by shrubs and it shimmered like an oasis. "Can we, can we?" we begged. "Absolutely!" the woman smiled. My father pulled the bus around by the office and shut off the loud generator as the man with the keys plugged us in. Then he and his wife brought out a six- pack of beer, climbed aboard, and sat in the back as if they had known us all of our lives. The children all slipped on their swimsuits and ran for the pool. Even stuck in the shallow end, due to my inability to swim, I was glad to escape the heat of the bus.

We had another opportunity to jump in the water the next morning, prior to our departure. After the motel had emptied out of guests, our hosts said their good-byes and welcomed us back anytime. On Highway 17, just before Binghampton, the bus crawled up a winding hill and we pulled over frequently to let commuters by. Ominous, bruise-colored clouds formed behind us as we approached the sunlit hills of the summit ahead. We were all looking forward to the glide awaiting us on the downhill slope, but the bus was straining and the temperature gage was in the red. We pulled over at a scenic vista on the summit to let the vehicle cool. However, Dad could not get it started again, and soon the dark clouds enveloped the summit and us along with it. Large drops of rain and hail clicked and popped on the roof and windshield. Suddenly, there was silence. The generator had stopped, the wind strengthened, and panic soon set in. Lightning crackled all around us and when a tree exploded outside my mother's window, she started to cry. Dad began barking orders: "Joe Pat, cover the generator with the tent, Michael get ready to take your mother's chest-piece off because we are going to have to manually crank the rocking bed to conserve the battery." We all flew into action and soon Michael, Joe Pat, and I were taking turns cranking the bed as David cried and Patrick stared at the tempest outside. Meme, riveted to her chair, watched in silence as my father rubbed my mother's hand and consoled her. When the storm passed, we all looked at one another in astonishment and relief. Joe Pat put the chest-piece back on, Dad poured water into the radiator, the generator was revved up again, and we pushed the bus down the hill to get it jump-started. As we snaked through down-town Binghampton, New York, everyone remained silent, including David, until my mother remarked, "I feel better now, can we pull over for a scotch?"

That night we camped in Friendship, a town close to the Pennsylvania border. It was Sunday when we awoke, and my father started looking for a Catholic Church to attend Mass. "Surely, your God would not mind if you missed church this once," Meme grumbled. Dad did not even look at her to respond; his devotion came first, and he loved attending Mass. A supporting chorus to his search, we children were commiserating over the prospect of having a mortal sin blacken our immortal souls. Dying with a mortal sin guaranteed eternal hell, and that was a risk too dire to take. We tried to avoid venial sins when we could, but it was difficult, because swearing, fighting, and being late for Mass were all inevitable. Widening our margin of excuses for those small transgressions was the knowledge that Purgatory, no matter how painful, would be temporary. Eternity, in contrast, was unfathomable. To our dismay, it was ten o'clock and we had not yet found a church. "Dad, we are going to be late," Michael complained. My father rolled his eyes and continued driving. "If you make us late, it's your sin, not mine," I announced. Dad looked at me and stated: "it is not a sin if you don't have sufficient reflection and full consent of the will!" I was puzzled by the statement, but felt relieved that I did not have to bring the matter up with Father Anthony the next time I went to confession. We finally arrived at a church, and though the service had already started, we ambled in and found a pew up front - conspicuously late and strange to the congregation. Dad was not shy about his Latin responses, and his voice echoed over the timid and mumbling voices of the parishioners. Joe Pat, Michael, and I felt the tension in the church and in the eyes of the catholics of Friendship, whose Sunday obligation, a perfunctory exercise, did not rise to my father's level of exuberance. When he beat his chest during the Mea Culpa he did so with passion and when he sang his voice rattled the stained-glass windows. When the Mass ended, my father approached the priest and asked if my mother could receive Communion. The Father agreed, but the Eucharist trembled in his fingers as he placed the wafer on my mother's tongue, obviously affected by the disruption of his Sunday ritual. We left after Communion, kicking up dust in the dirt parking lot, while the stunned congregation gawked in silent amazement.

Queenie

Chapter Fourteen - Meadville and Back

En route to Meadville
(left to right: Bernie, Patrick, and David)

As the bus made its way through the back roads of New York and Pennsylvania on the way to Route 6, even the roar of the generator could not mask the quiet. Mom was thinking about our arrival in Meadville, and all the friends and relatives there who would react to her new physical circumstances. No one from Meadville had seen her since she contracted polio, and she understood that the inability to make physical contact, or even gesture, heightened the awkwardness. Out her window she could see the rolling, green foothills before entering the Alleghany Mountains. The colors of grey, green, and blue created a moving reflection in her glasses. She had been the chipper new bride with an English accent during her last time in Pennsylvania. She had played tennis, waded in the streams and hiked the mountains, and now the best she could hope for was the ability to observe and to talk. No one could understand how her happiness persisted. Tired words like "plucky" and "courageous", when used to describe her, seemed inappropriate because she did not feel particularly brave. She said that she listened to music differently now, allowing the violins, cellos, and lutes to rouse her emotions--often crying happily to a passage. "You need to hear this!" she would command. "Sit down and turn it up." She greeted everyone cheerfully, and she was genuinely ecstatic to see them. Other people made possible the lively conversations, animated games of cards, or rounds of Scrabble that kept her spirits up. Solemnly, someone would ask: "What do you miss the most?" "Easy," she'd reply, "beating the children!" If someone was walking by, she would often stick her tongue out at them just to get a reaction. And yet, even when her eyeglasses were crooked, she retained her dignity, and the glint in her eyes challenged any signs of pity or sympathy.

When we pulled up to Limber Road and the farm our five cousins, Uncle Joe and Aunt Mary came rushing out the front door. As they stepped onto the bus, Marie announced, "Joe, Mary, I want a kiss," with tears of joy steaming down her cheeks. Soon everyone stood around her bed talking; she asked all the questions, and by doing so, she set everyone at ease. A large meal was being planned by the adults as the children investigated the farm. We were fascinated by the chickens, roosters, and Joker, the milking cow who had been born on April 1st two years earlier. My father drove the bus onto their front lawn, as close to the front porch as possible, and we plugged in.

In the morning, mist clung over the cornfield, by the dirt road. From the back window of the bus, I remember feeling a strong urge to explore, as I stared out at the swaying trees and fields to the horizon while the farm slowly stirred to life. A formidable elm tree partially blocked the old, graying barn, and underneath it, chickens pecked at the ground. More aging elms dotted the opposite hill. Where the backyard sloped down to a small stream, tiny birds chirped and hovered. Blink, the loveable, black-and-white mixed breed, sat in front of his dog-house, patiently waiting for food. Everyone had stayed up very late the night before and were sleeping. David woke first and he felt obliged to wake everyone in the bus because he was hungry. Despite their fatigue, everyone seemed quietly cheerful as they roused. Our goal was to visit Arch Street, where Grandma Mulligan would be waiting with Sister James Francis, for an early lunch. Grandma entered the bus with her flowered apron and cooking utensils, clapping her hands together with glee. Mom's smile was as wide as she could make it. Sister James Francis and my grandmother were both great talkers, and they were especially motivated because my mother had requested a dissertation on the Mulligan Family and its history. Sister was the scribe, and she sat in Meme's chair writing proficiently as her mother wove one tale after another. "Did you know that my grandmother's neighbor shot and killed a trespasser?" Grandma asked. She surveyed the astonished faces around her, waved her hand, and then slapped her knee. "Well, it's true!" she announced excitedly, and drew everyone into the story. My mother, who was sipping tea, cheered her on with gasps and chuckles, so delighted in the amity. The bus was full of children who were not the least bit enthralled, but listened intently anyway, hoping that soon the bus would embark to the swimming hole. After the visit we were headed for Prather's at Woodcock Creek, to a pool under a bridge where the water was deep, and there were three four-foot-high telephone poles protruding from the bank.

Marie invited Sister and Grandma to accompany us to the swimming hole. Their conversation had to compete with the noise of the bus. We pulled up to the grass turnaround past the bridge, to ensure that my mother could watch as we dove off the telephone poles. The current flowed gently, the water was clear, and the rounded rocks that coated the bottom seemed to shift shape below the rippling surface. One could easily dive horizontally into the flow, glide to the sandy bank on the other side, run up the bank, cross the bridge, and climb on top of the poles once again. As the afternoon turned to dusk we continued our drill. The tops of the poles became soggy, and as I stood onto the pole, pushing off, I slipped into the current below. I could not swim. I sank to the stones and held my breath creeping and paddling across the bottom. I felt panic and my movements became hysterical; I was flailing away on the bottom of the river. Just when I could hold my breath no longer, I felt a strong hand pick me up under my armpit. I gasped when I surfaced. Uncle Joe had seen me, and pulled me up. As he carried me to the other side, he whispered, "You can't swim?" "No, Uncle Joe, I can't," I sadly admitted. "All Mulligans can swim. Come with me," he said. He ushered me to a calm pool on the other side of the bridge and had me hold onto a large, smooth boulder. After I mastered floating, he showed me the frog-kick, and within thirty minutes, I had mastered the breast-stroke. That summer all I ever wanted to do was to swim.

My mother was having the best summer of her post-polio life. Uncle Ed and Aunt Audrey were coming over for a picnic and Marie beamed with excitement. Every day the planning would start early in the morning--picnics and swimming excursions for twenty people ranging in age from 5 years to 70, required lists, time schedules, and responsibilities. Lines formed at the foot of my mother's rocking bed as each individual waited to discuss his or her role in the plan. Since our arrival, my father had been going out with his brother Joe at night, and they frequently did not return at the pre-designated time. As a result, despite my father's role as the key implementer of our plans, he was no longer involved in the process of decision-making. He was in the doghouse. And yet, Mom and Dad were quite close in

Meadville, often staring into each other's face, inches apart, whispering and kissing. The time there strengthened the desire for happiness she had previously thought impossible. Dad's residence in the doghouse was handled playfully by my mother, who often called him an "Old Goat." She knew that he would show up almost on time, just like he did when he visited her every day for three years in the hospital. Occasionally, he would have had a little too much to drink and would say something wicked. More than anyone, my father constituted a critical component of her happiness, because he was the only one who could attend to her every need and he had demonstrated his willingness to be there for her. In fact, it was he who had convinced her that life was worth living during the darkest moments in Chapin Hospital. She would periodically test his resolve; "I'm just a burden to you all!" she would sulk, requisitioning the calming remark of "That's not true, honey!"

The morning we departed Meadville, we all cried. The time spent on the farm with our cousins, aunts, and uncles passed so quickly. Running with Blink the dog, feeding the animals, swimming in the many creeks, and exploring the woods had consumed every moment for Michael, our cousins, and me. Eating, sleeping, and visiting with grown-ups were only distractions from the games of army or baseball. We knew that we had to leave eventually, but the thought never truly surfaced until the night before departure. As we sat on the bus, rumbling down the dirt road with tears running all over our faces, my father looked straight ahead. His pipe was empty, but it moved up and down in his jaw like a metronome. Joe Pat stayed behind, and he was sorely missed on the long ride home. Michael bickered with me and Patrick bickered with David, and my father interceded more than once to settle us down. We arrived home, put my mother on a stretcher, and carried her in through the front door.

The following day, she watched the tall willow tree out her window bending in the breeze. She knew it so well: its inhabitants, its shape, its season. She listened to Vaughn Williams' 'Fantasia on a Theme' on the record player. She told us to listen to the instruments as they countered one another, and pretend that we were listening to a conversation. As a single violin responded pleadingly to a quartet, the change in tempo and mood mimicked a discussion that increased in intensity. While the fervor of the music heightened, my mother's eyes fixated on the tree outside the window. Her vision, made acute by being cemented in one place at every moment, allowed her to absorb so much more than any of the rest of us.

Mom turned her head toward us as the music faded. "Do you see what I mean?" she asked. "When there are no lyrics, the music needs to be even more expressive." I sat in the easy chair, worn smooth from the years of shifting posteriors on its faded orange upholstery. David was sitting on the left side of my mother's bed, with his lower back resting against the mattress and his rear on the wooden foot rest. Patrick occupied the right side, legs dangling, watching TV without sound. Michael was on the desk chair, next to the television, digesting with me the music we just heard. The piece had lasted about twenty minutes. "It was more of a debate," I said, even though my mind had wandered during the performance. "I see what you mean," Michael replied, "Still, I'd rather listen to the Beach Boys." My mother turned her head and continued her perusal of the tree as my father came into the room. "I'd rather listen to a toilet flush!" he scoffed. My mother turned to him glaringly. "I mean rather than listen to the Beach Boys," he blurted defensively, though she understood what he had meant. He was teasing, but she had noticed change in her husband. She knew when something was wrong. The slump of my father's shoulders made her sad, all the more because she was powerless to relieve the burden to any great extent. His increasing unhappiness is clearly evident in the diary entry at that time. He would admit I am sure that the fact he was venting may have caused some exaggeration. He wrote:

"I have become more and more averse to doing anything except drinking. Even writing in this diary is difficult. I hate to write letters, to take baths. I hate nursing. If it weren't for the work that Michael and Bernie do I would never get through. There is hardly an evening when relaxation is the order of

the day. Shopping, Boy Scouts, Cub Scouts, splash party, birthday party, church at St. Margaret's and at St. Brenden's, rubber check from Burke Healy, funerals, weddings, anniversaries, took both TV's to the repair shop, growth curves, get Marie set up for the day, baths, rubdowns, adjustments, 5 cats with two cat pans to clean."

Yet, he had time to run the chorus at the Veteran's hospital and at church, and he would volunteer to play piano or the organ at functions for St. Margaret's School. The unexpected was what overwhelmed him, usually when one of my mother's attendants would call in sick, or if the car failed. The rest of the time he laughed and joked, listened to music and played the Baldwin piano in his room. He even gave us lessons. He coached our Little League baseball teams and loved the fact that we were avid players. In his diary, one can feel his sense of pride as he describes the day that Michael, a catcher for the Rumford Lions, had been rundown at home plate by the burly Tom McGrath, but he still managed to tag him out and hold onto the ball. What he did not find the time for was paperwork; he failed to fill out and mail federal tax forms for 1959, 1960, or 1961, and he often forgot to renew his driver's license, a potentially inconvenient issue whenever we got stopped.

In 1962, Meme asked me if I wanted to come and live with her for a while in England. I was enthusiastic and my parents agreed because Michael had refused the invitation. My mother wanted us to see England the country she missed so much. She wanted to introduce us to her family. In time, both Patrick and David also visited Meme in England.

Chapter Fifteen - England

Meme (left), Hilde(right) and Bernie in England

As I stared out the window of the BOAC Jet, the lights of Boston shone like candles below and I began to cry. I was 11 years old, and my parents were sending me to England to live for four months. I had been an enthusiastic participant in the planning and execution of the adventure. But now, as Boston, my family, friends, and the game of baseball shrunk in my mind's eye, I was overcome with sadness. Bournemouth, England, and Meme were 10 hours away. I looked at the middle-aged man sitting next to me, stubbing his cigarette out in the ash tray burrowed in the armrest in between us. I watched it smolder in its metal casing. I snapped the lid for him as the smoke stung my tearful, reddened eyes. He reached up and pressed a button, then looked down at me. "You seem very sad," he said smiling. "Is this your first time flying?" I shook my head. I had adopted a policy of not talking to strange grown-ups, especially if they smoked cigarettes. Suddenly, a woman with bright reddish purple hair curled around a cap appeared over his shoulder. She smiled broadly and I admired the sparkling gold button on the lapel of her jacket, depicting a magnificent winged horse. "England is quite lovely, you'll see," she chirped. "Do they play baseball there?" I queried, sniffling. "Do you have any Kleenex?" I added. "No and yes," she replied giggling. I wondered why these people reflexively laughed and smiled about my sadness. I returned to the window and subverted my sorrow by gazing at the shadow of the plane, silhouetted by moonlight, on the clouds.

I slept most of the way. However, as we started our landing, I viewed England's sumptuous green earth between wisps of white clouds. Mesmerized by the sight, I lost my homesickness. Meme picked me up at the airport, and we took a cab to the train station. Ornate buildings of marble and granite dwarfed the busy streets. Each new person I met was immediately aware of my accent, and each responded with the identical remark, "Yank, eh!" I knew what they meant, but at the time, any affiliation inferred about the New York Yankees roiled me. Meme was dressed impeccably that day, with a black feather cap on her silver hair and a waist length black coat draped over a pale grey dress. The outfit seemed to broaden her shoulders. She seemed so glamorous. The deep gold locket hanging on a formidable chain blended like a mosaic against the grey dress. She had applied lipstick subtly. I had never seen Meme this way. I was intimidated somewhat. Meme's eyes were large and the color of chestnuts. They scanned the world around her. "Isn't it lovely," Meme exclaimed as we gaped at the English countryside from the windows of the train. "I wish you all lived here. You'd be much better for it!"

Meme's house in Bournemouth was decorated with beds of flowers in the front and a vegetable garden in the back, and it contrasted surreally with the house on Ruth Avenue. I had my own bedroom and a king-sized bed replaced the army cot I was accustomed to. One could hear the ticking of a six-foot high, pendulum-driven grandfather clock at the bottom of the stairs. Meme would turn her color television on for one hour each night. My young mind could not grasp the humor of the foreign programs she watched, but hearing her chuckle delighted me. I played tennis with my cousins at an affluent club, and although nothing could replace baseball, I enjoyed dressing in white and competing.

"Come on, Bernie," Meme chirped up the stairs. "Tea at Rebecca Simmons's house." As we walked to her house ten blocks away Meme, briefed me on deportment and cautioned me about Mrs. Simmons. "She spits when she talks so you musn't sit too close. She is quite daft, so if you don't understand her just smile and nod." Meme stopped me on the sidewalk to demonstrate. She smiled and gave a subtle nod. Nevertheless, when Rebecca Simmons began rambling, Meme caught my attention and she rolled her eyes dramatically, while maintaining a beatific smile outwards. Meme was so kind to Rebecca, invigorating her conversation with questions and exclamations. When Mrs. Simmons left to get the tea and fruitcake, Meme looked at me and raised her cloth napkin to dab at each fictional drop of saliva. She punctuated the skit with a query, "Is my make-up running?" When Rebecca returned carrying the tea precariously on her silver tray, I could not contain myself. Rebecca looked at Meme. "What's he laughing at?" "Something we saw on the telly last night," Meme answered smoothly. On the way back to her house, Meme recalled the events of the afternoon tea as we laughed and giggled together. Before we got to the house Meme commented, "She is really quite nice, don't you think?"

I returned to America having been exposed to affluence and quiet. I had missed my friends and baseball but found it difficult to sleep on an army cot with Michael two feet away. Beans and franks and TV Dinners could not replace the whitefish with Meme's home-made wine sauce. There was no color television at Ruth Avenue. We had a 14" black and white TV and I had to endure endless competition as to what we'd be watching. I had to wash dishes for a week to earn the right to watch The Beatles play on Ed Sullivan.

Chapter Sixteen

"Quite Solemn."

Michael and I sat across from each other in our respective easy chairs. Our arms rested on the small coffee table that separated us. "You ready?" he asked with quiet intensity. "Yup!" I replied confidently. We sat motionless except for the movement of our heads and one index finger. After a minute or two Michael broke the silence. "How can you stand it?" he asked rolling his eyes in amazement. "What?" I responded defensively. "There's a booger or something in your nose." "No suh!" I barked at him. He smiled smugly as the thought of a something in my nose burrowed into my brain. Only two minutes passed before my stamina evaporated, and I reached up and squeezed my nose. I had lost the waiting game of polio and my fifty cents again. The only consolation left to me was the knowledge that I could always try again; polio wasn't about to get up and leave us.

Elm Stump

In 1963, my parents decided to spruce up the yard. The backyard was all sand and gravel with miniature dry stream beds that filled up when it rained. The septic system on the left was surrounded by the only grass capable of growing. My father remedied this by purchasing several bales of hay and spreading them around the backyard. Soon, the backyard was green. However, it was difficult to cut, so Michael and I would be dispatched with scythes to swing back and forth until the stiff stalks of hay were an inch and a half high. It wasn't the kind of lawn that one could lay on. Hurricane Donna knocked down our elm tree in the front yard. The tree was cut, leaving a four foot stump, and asphalt was poured all around it. They installed a 3 ½ foot deep swimming pool on the asphalt. On the first day of swimming, Michael dove from the stump into the water and cracked his head open. As he came up bleeding from the bottom, I wondered how many procedures and policies would need to be put in place to avoid such a calamity from occurring again in the future. Much to the delight of our seven cats, my mother decided to put a bird bath on top of the stump, and instituted a no diving policy. It didn't take long for the asphalt to cause fissures in the bottom of the pool, which eventually ruptured—flooding the blacktop, and draining into the backyard now protected by hay. Several layers of padding were placed on the tarmac before the pool was fitted with a new rubber bottom. The no diving policy stayed in place. A metal fence was placed around the front yard with a gate opening to the refurbished slate walkway.

On a spring day that year, during a thunderstorm, we jumped off the school bus and scurried down the sidewalk. We stopped at the gate to see my father sitting placidly in a chair in the front yard, his pipe cradled in his hand, looking out at the McNulty's yard. He was soaked, but he was seemingly oblivious to his condition. I entered the side door to see my mother crying and muttering to herself. My father had run the big grey Buick into another car, totaling it, although the Buick was unscathed. When the police came, they discovered that my father's license had expired and some previous infractions of his had gone unattended. He was also cited for drunk driving. Doris, my mother's attendant at the time, had to fetch him from the East Providence Police station, and when he arrived home he had to confess the whole incident to my mother. My father had desperately escaped into the gloomy storm as my mother honed in on his transgressions, reviling them one by one. Dad, grasping for a position amongst his obvious and numerous blunders, argued that his life at home had become unbearable. The chaos brought about by the unending presence of so many occupants, vendors, animals, visitors, and passers-by, cluttered the house and led him to drink. "When could I ever find the place or time or quiet that I need to fill out the forms to renew my license?" he said. "This place is a zoo!" That's when he left to sit in the rain. As the dust settled, a deal was struck. My father would quit drinking if the house became more peaceful.

Peace would be achieved by eliminating the constant flow of children, vendors, and neighborhood animals from the house. As I stood next to my mother's bed and she explained all this, we both stared at my father sitting motionless on the chair in the pouring rain. A day or two later, the deal was modified to allow my father to drink beer, and like a crack forming in a hastily built dam, the flood of humans and animals soon resumed. The blaring of competing radios and record players filled the house again. My father had realized that when he was alone with my mother in the peace he craved, he was responsible for every bed pan, every meal, and every itch once Doris left for the day. If our friends could not come over, then we would spend all our time outside, and out of his reach. Similarly, my mother discovered that a completely sober dad was better, but she was addicted to the chaos as much as he was to his beer.

Every weekend of that summer, we would drive with many neighborhood children, including Michael's new girlfriend, Phyllis, to Lincoln Woods for fresh water swimming or to Lido's beach and the ocean. Meme returned from England, and we drove to Meadville in August. We took the same route as our first trip, stopping at the L&M Motel and in Jamestown, New York. This time, the traveling went more smoothly. It was the year of songs about summer, surfing, and cars. Michael and I listened to our 45's as much as we could. We had purchased a record player at Apex Department Store with the money we had earned from paper routes, caddying, and our allowance. On the bus, at night, we'd spin songs for anyone who wanted to listen. *Surfer Joe* by The Surfaris was our favorite at the time, because of its story-line about a surfer who is forced to cut his hair and conform after landing in the army. We watched a lot of the older punks, gangsters, and losers in our neighborhood subdued by their entry into the army or marines, and the song appealed to us. My favorite music was Peter, Paul, and Mary, and the Kingston Trio. My mother and father both liked the new folk music, and I could play rudimentary versions of the songs for them on my Kay Guitar. However, on the bus, we only played 45's, drumming along with *Wipe Out* or wailing to *Don't Worry Baby*. When we arrived in Jamestown, New York, we decided to stay with my father's cousins who we referred to as "Aunts", because of their demure behavior. Ann was serious, and concerned about etiquette and appearance. Gert, alternatively, was one of the most cheerful, almost blissful, humans I have ever met. Their mother, Aunt Mary, lived with them. She was ruled by a sense of distinctive, proper conduct. She was in love with a male tenant of hers, but could not marry him for fear of upsetting the careful agenda of propriety.

Their house was built on a very steep hill, with two levels of basement and two floors above. From the alley at the bottom of the hill facing the back of the house, one could almost feel gravity pulling at the house and its cables and clotheslines. The bus was parked by the bottom of the hill, next to the alley, and far from the prying eyes of neighbors. Michael and I were relegated to the top basement with our record player, while Patrick, David, Meme, Mom, and Dad occupied the bus. My mother entertained my aunts with deep, contemplative discussion of literature. Dad could only tolerate the piety so much before wisecracking: "Is that what Tennyson was trying to say? I thought he was describing the state of his gastro-intestinal tract!" This outburst of sarcasm perturbed my mother and Ann, but Gert could not stop laughing. "Bernard," my mother replied sternly. She was angry because he would only behave this badly when he had a beer or two. Gert continued laughing, and Dad was willing to suffer the consequence for the satisfaction of making her laugh. Mom stopped her lecture before it began, yet she did not forget it. As my father was putting my mother to bed, she chose her moment. "I don't joke about your church music," she said. "There's nothing funny about church music," he replied. "We sometimes refer to it as solemn." "You don't think there is anything solemn about Tennyson!" she cracked with a smile. "That's what so funny about it!" he relented, disintegrating into laughter. My mother soon joined him, and they took the solemn theme as far as it would go. The "solemn" joke went on for years afterward between them. If I moped they'd frequently inquire; "Bernie, why so solemn?"

We arrived in Meadville to the same excitement as the years

before. Joker, the cow, was accompanied by a new cow, and there were even more chickens and cats with no names in and around the barn. Michael was turning 15 in a few days, I was 12. The gentle stream that ran behind the barn enchanted us--it featured sandy banks, tiny islands, newts, frogs, and minnows. We had all just completed our chores; weeding the long rows of corn, cleaning the chicken coop, and milking the cows seemed to encompass the whole of "Uncle Joe's Farm Summer Experience". Dad had an 8mm movie camera that he pointed at everyone. Most of the movies consisted of startled faces and the shrinking size of human forms as they ran away from the lens. My mother sat in the bus with a constant flow of visitors, as usual. Looking out her window at the barn, the cows and the tufts of trees in the fields stretched picturesquely towards the horizon, she imagined shaking a blanket and placing it on the green earth. She watched as we ran down the hill, scattering chickens, as we disappeared behind the barn towards the stream. Our cousins, Tom and Terry, were constant instigators around the farm and were partners with us on all our adventures. Michael, Tom, Terry, and I scampered to the sandy border of the stream to find frogs, newts, and other amphibious wildlife. We settled to rest under a large oak tree.

The tree beckoned into the sky; its many branches spiraled upwards in what we saw as an invitation to climb. Terry started up first. For each branch he reached, we scurried up after him, each of us vying for a branch atop the rest. Silently we contended, the rustling of branches playing like the score to our competition. After ten minutes or so, Michael was furthest up the tree by far. Suddenly, a loud snap came from above. We all jerked to attention, to watch Michael tumble through the branches and land in the stream. As he lay in a heap, abjectly moaning, I clambered cautiously down the tree and ran to get my father. I found him in the bus, smoking his pipe and listening to Aunt Mary and my mother. I blurted the news and he ran down the hill immediately. I was quickly interrogated by my mother and aunt; "He fell out of a tree!" was my only reply. My mother stared out the window as Michael, who was hanging on to my father, came into view. His face was distorted in pain and his steps were short. His right arm stuck horizontally out from his shoulder, and his swollen, misshapen elbow dangled with his forearm swinging gently like a pendulum. The closer he got to the bus, the more frantic my mother became. Her voice began as a whisper and crescendoed into a scream, "Oh my God, Michael!" My father placed Michael into Uncle Joe's car, then ran into the bus and assured my mother that the injury wasn't as bad as it looked. "How do you know?" she snapped, as she started crying. My father rolled his eyes, lowered himself out of the bus, and jumped into the car. Uncle Joe's tires spun in the dirt as he sped away. Aunt Mary and Meme gathered around my mother's bed consoling and reassuring her. Tom, Terry, and I returned to the scene of the incident, murmuring amongst ourselves about which branch had failed.

Michael returned several hours later with his arm in a cast and shoulder cradled in a sling. He had broken his wrist, as well as dislocated his elbow and collarbone. The next day, while we were sitting on the bus, we wrote on his cast as my mother sipped tea. Dad sat in the driver's seat while Michael reveled in his sudden, painful celebrity. Recalling the descent, he raised his healthy hand and pointed upward, from there he drew a dramatic line down to describe the fall; "It was like slow motion," he said, "I could feel the lower branches slapping me as I fell." "Well, you could have broken your neck," my father cautioned, cleaning blackened tobacco out of his pipe with a pen knife. "I couldn't even help him!" my mother stated ruefully, as her voice quavered and she looked out her window at the barn. Tears welled up in her eyes. "I can't help him now," she lamented. Our collective focus shifted from Michael to my mother. My father got out of his seat, walked purposefully over to her, took her glasses off and after he wiped the steam from the lenses, he placed his hand on hers and whispered something to her. She gazed at him and tearfully shook her head with a weak smile. Michael left the bus, having been upstaged again. "Yes, quite solemn," she murmured, watching the chickens pecking at the earth.

Chapter Seventeen - Fish Sticks

Providence

Oblivious to being followed, Michael sailed along on his commute to school. Dad had inadvertently sighted him where Angell Street touched Meeting Street. This incited his curiosity, and he edged along behind. As he drove, he must have been thinking about his son's transition to adulthood. "He excels at his studies, yet he's clearly not happy in school," my father had pondered in his diary. The fact that Mike received a scholarship for full tuition at St. Raphael's Academy was the primary reason for his attendance at the expensive all-boys secondary school. Michael's understanding of mathematics was effortless, and he had already completed calculus in the ninth grade. The relationship between Mike and our parents was purely functional at best, devoid of laughter and camaraderie. As the oldest, he was leaned on heavily to manage the rest of us once our mother could not. Suddenly at the age of seven, he was cooking, ironing, hanging up clothes, washing dishes, and completing any task that we were too young or too short to perform. He was trusted with money, often paying for deliveries and for milk. Now, he was studying, preparing for college, working, and dating Phyllis. When Michael graduated from Saint Margaret's my father wrote:

"Michael's graduation went off in splendid fashion. We were happily shocked to hear his reward for rank second--scholarship to St. Ray's. Johnny Barnes and Wayne Tracy were tied for first. Mike's average was only .03 under theirs. According to Marie I have been too sparing in my praise for Mike, who said during the event: "At last I made Dad proud of me!". I guess maybe I'm too reticent and should have told him of other times when I was proud, like when he caught for the Lions and had such a fighting spirit and threw men out on base to win games. Especially, I remember one terrific peg to third to Louis Carotta when Louis tagged the runner's foot just as it was ready to touch the base. It was the third out and it won the game for the Lions. I'm proud every time he walks out on the altar to serve and especially I'm proud of the way he pitches in at home. This may take some urging but he does it and does it well. I was proud when he earned the Ad Altare Dei award--he was the only one in the troop to earn it that year. I'm proud that he is just Michael."

Despite my parents' apparent understanding of the meaning of praise it did not change the discourse very much. "Michael, call the fire department and remind them to bring the generator because the electricity has been off." "Michael, give Patrick a dollar for ice cream, I'll pay you back." "Michael, your father is at Three Twigs but won't come to the phone so you will need to go get him." In his diary, my father wrote a reaction to one of Doris's tirades that conveyed his appreciation: "she irritated me by criticizing Michael for being lazy and quoted examples of other boys--I told her I didn't care about them. I thought to myself how they would make out in a home similarly equipped with difficulties!" Unfortunately, Mike did not have the benefit of reading Dad's diaries so he was unaware of his sentiments.

Michael's desire to associate with Ruth Avenue decreased significantly as a teenager, and coincided with the increase in my father's drinking. Dad's drinking changed his personality dramatically, yet to him it seemed a necessary evil in order to deal with the burden most days carried. The endless chaos of his life was chronicled in his logs. A slew of disappointments beset him year after year; the failure of water pumps, spark plugs, and other nuisances with the bus, the inconvenient scheduling of funerals, weddings, and Masses, struggles with bosses and co-workers, the insane nature of his home, limited free time, and the complexities of my mother's needs, all drove him to escape more and more to alcohol. With my Beatle haircut, conspiracy theories, and budding rock and roll lifestyle, I was also getting on my father's nerves. Presumably in connection with his high level of stress, he developed asthma that he characterized as "crippling." To our stream of visitors, my mother offered food, tea, and coffee to everyone. Beyond the community of family, friends, and neighbors, our pet population had burgeoned to nine cats. Dad had to siphon cash from his church jobs to fund his trips to the bar, and to buy newspapers and tobacco for his pipe. Mom and Dad would frequently argue about money or fret in unison.

The atmosphere of our home was erratic. While our mother

might be chatty and sanguine, our father could be sullen and create dissonance. Conversely, he found temporary highs through drinking that occasionally might bring him up, while her mood plummeted in disappointment. The combination of those factors, a limited family income and an unpredictable home life, led Michael and me to search the outside world for financial stability. Michael and I initially made our own money with paper routes and caddying at the golf course. Later, Michael got a job at Davol Rubber and purchased a car. It was the summer of 1965; I was 14 years old, and Michael was on the verge of turning 17. Michael was rarely home. During his time with Phyllis and her family he had glimpsed a life of normalcy, and found it preferable to what passed for ordinary at Ruth Avenue.

I walked through the side door past the kitchen table and glanced at my mother's reflection. I passed the refrigerator and reached above it to retrieve my glasses, hidden there earlier that morning on my way to school. I slipped the glasses on, sharpening my vision, but as I self-consciously knew, detracting from my appearance. "Hi, Mom," I smiled as I passed the door of her room. Ma was working on my father's composition of a three-day lecture series for the Carnegie Institute, *Anti-microbial Agents and Techniques and Methods in the Diagnosis of Tuberculosis*. Mom and Dad were a formidable writing team and this endeavor invigorated their interaction. Dad would present the facts to her as he was putting her to bed or when he was setting her up for tea. "Misplaced modifier!" she would say. "Poetic license!" he would counter. The collaboration buoyed my mother's mood. So involved was she in the project that she hardly noticed me in the mirror. I scurried up the stairs to my room, evading enlistment, and found my record player. I fell on my army cot and stared at the bulging folds of insulation tucked between the beams of wood that served as the ceiling. Opening my window, I relaxed in the gentle sadness of "Warmth of the Sun," by the Beach Boys.

When I awoke it was dusk, and I heard the side door under my window slam. Dad was home. I decided to remain quiet in my room until I was called to dinner. Soon my parents' voices echoed up the stairway; an unexpected anguish was present in the shared tone. The door to my father's room slammed after his loud announcement: "I have some reading to do!". "Bernie?" my mother whispered through the intercom on my wall. I walked down the stairs and into her room. I stood at the foot of my mother's bed, reaching instinctively for her feet to placate her. She told me to put the fish-sticks in the oven and heat it to 375 degrees for fifteen minutes. Patrick and David were at the table already playing a game of Sorry. Michael was at Phyllis's house. While I set the table, Patrick retrieved the ketchup and tartar sauce from the refrigerator. Peas from a can accompanied the fish once it was ready. The black and white television that usually accompanied the conversation was the only sound, other than the scraping of utensils and the chewing of food. My mother was quietly looking out her window. The house was so uncharacteristically still, except for the hum of my mother's respirator that I could actually hear the clock ticking on the wall.

After they finished their meal, Patrick and David retreated to their room to continue their game. I sat sullenly at the table having eaten only the peas. The fish-sticks languished on my plate with only one small bite evident. Dry and tasteless, the fish had no appeal to me and I was not hungry. My father's door opened and I could hear his labored breathing as he walked down the hall past the bathroom. As he put food on his plate he asked, "Aren't you going to eat your dinner?" I didn't answer. He stood for only a moment at the stove, put his plate down, and raised his hand. Slapping me on the back of my head, he hissed through clenched teeth, "Answer me when I ask you a question." I felt a welt rising where his wedding ring had landed. My mother yelled from her room for him to stop, shocked. "When I put food on the table," he muttered, "I expect…" he stopped in mid-sentence as I stood up. I reached into my pocket, pulled out five dollars and dropped it on top of my food. "That should cover it," I said sarcastically. I started to walk to the upstairs, but he caught up with me in the living room. He grabbed my arm and turned me around to face him. By this time, I could hear my mother crying uncontrollably. I finally looked him in the eyes. It was as if I was looking at him for the first time in years. His green eyes swimming in red, his hair graying, and his jaw locked around his unlit pipe. He took his pipe out and stood unsteadily. "You think you're a man, don't you?". I could not reply. The torment of his life, the unyielding pain and frustration of his often futile existence revealed itself to me for the very first time. I glanced back through the mirror at my mother as she said, "Michael, go help Bernie." Michael had arrived back early from the Gentile's house. Whatever peace my brother had achieved there was abruptly shattered. I looked back at Dad and began to cry. Michael wedged himself between us. Suddenly, my father punched him in the forehead. Michael looked furiously at him. "Don't ever do that again!" Michael grasped Dad's shoulders firmly and led him into the bedroom. As he led him away he looked scornfully at me and cursed, "You fucking baby!" I ran up to my room and punched a hole in the flimsy wall. Michael called Pat Kralik to come over to put my mother to bed. When Michael came up to my room later that night in a conciliatory mood, he asked, "What was that all about?" Lying on my bed, I replied, "I didn't eat the stupid fish-sticks." Michael chuckled derisively. As he walked away I heard him mutter, "I am so sick of this."

Chapter Eighteen - Marie Speaks

"Emotions are my only movement now--they dance inside, billowing fantastically like the wind."

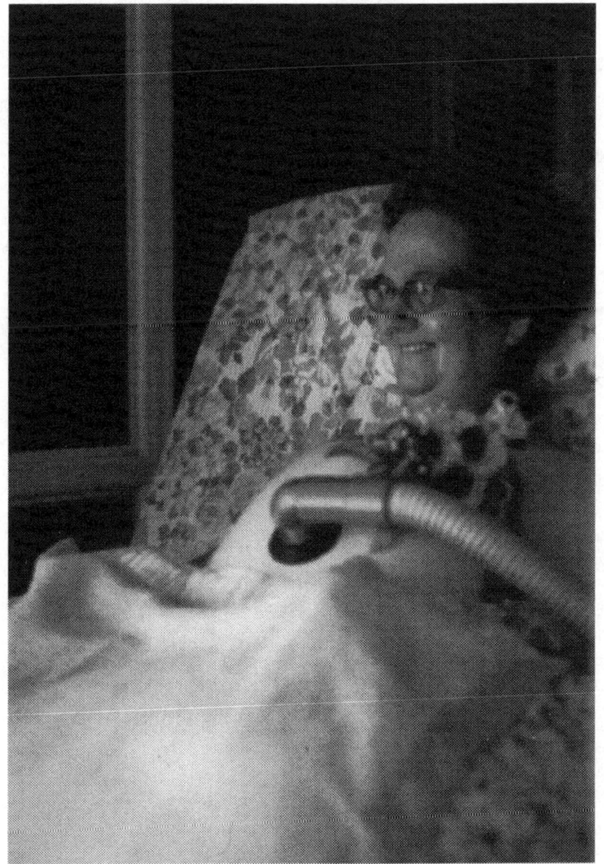

Portrait of Marie Mulligan

The glossy sand peels itself backwards with each receding wave; the gentle noise is blissful. The cliffs of the Isle of Wight are exposed over the edge of a soft cloud enveloping the island. I begin to walk; with my first step I am ungainly and struggling--long splints are fastened down the length of my legs.

Rising abruptly like a bubble to the surface of my awareness, the sound of my name picks me up and carries me away. I open my eyes to the view of the television at the foot of my bed, only to have it disappear as the rocking bed collapses down. On my return upwards, I notice how disheveled and unsteady Bernard appears, fumbling for the lotion and the bedpan, repeating my name once more to confirm that I am awake. These days, he walks around the house so dejectedly, an unhappy ghost in temper and tone. Last night's argument solidified my idea of his attitude as a surrender--how insufferable--I am the one who should have given up long ago. He seems so tired; he wheezes with asthma as he says weakly, "Are you ready?" Before I can reply, he flips the switch off, then on, then off again, to bring the rocking bed to a stop in a horizontal position. Behind my knees, the mattress lifts while he turns the crank at the bottom of my bed. After securing the chest piece and adjusting my head, he closes both doors to the room. Silently, he bathes me, and I wonder if he is searching for something to say, too. Reflexively, I ask him to move Michael along out of the bathroom so that Bernie can get in. His blank face is more hurtful than any emotion. I wish he knew that this was my way of helping, my only way. He wordlessly follows my request. My mind shifts to Doris and her suspicion that her husband, Albert, is having an affair. Each day she brought with her usual conversation a new clue, and while she may not be ready to admit it aloud, I think we both knew how her investigation would end. Quickly, my mind returns to the boys; David and Patrick are having a petty argument over the cereal box. I announce to Michael that it is Bernie's turn to shower. Since he's only waiting for the bathroom now, and has finished eating, I ask Bernie to let Penny in. I can hear her at the side door, slowly ruining it. Every morning she straddles the screen door between her paws, letting the flies in and scratching at the wire. No one seems to be able to pry her off when she's curled around the door with her claws sunk in. When it suits her, she comes into the house, jumps on my bed, curls up on my lap, and dreams the afternoon away. I often wonder if they like me best for loving them without petting them. It used to bother me dreadfully, until I realized that perhaps it was their preference. She sometimes gazes at me with her one crossed eye. She rubs against my chest piece in a similar fashion to the furniture. Am I furniture? I think she knows better than that. "Patrick! It is David's turn to read!" My face prematurely begins to tense up, as I expect to mediate some new quarrel between the two of them. How they could be so different, at only thirteen months apart in age, is a mystery. Through the window, I see Doris opening the front gate and a brazen squirrel on the stump, drinking out of the bird-feeder. I urge him to leave; once the cats spot him, he's already lost. Poor Doris--leaving Albert may be for the best--she has a thyroid condition and he says such nasty things to her about her weight. I notice Bernard squeezing past her at the screen door as they change shifts. It breaks my heart to see his hunched shoulders as he ambles to the car, distracted. He takes with him his true confidante, his pipe. I reflect on the dull quiet when he bathed me, the absence in his eyes, and suddenly, I am brought back to Sugar Lake, years ago. For a brief moment I can sense the warmth between us then, swimming and laughing. The way that the glow of the campfires we had set up together colored our memories. I had always felt held by knowing the strength of his affection, even when he wasn't near, and even when I couldn't feel. What has happened to us? The children are slowly filing out of the house to school. I watch David limp along, unhappy to go. His expression seems thoughtful. I hear a wooden creak of submission as Doris sits in the chair beside me. "He admits it," she quavers. "Oh, Doris, I am so sorry," I start to comfort her but I wonder; what does this mean for her tenure here? I keep my thoughts to myself. As her tears flow and we talk, I wonder if she shouldn't be paying me for my therapeutic service. Yet, while she may not be able to cope with her own life, she is reliable. This makes the issue of her employment here all the more delicate--she is consistent, but not particularly helpful. Really, I think I need a younger woman, and perhaps a more cheerful one. Earlier, I had sent Michael to invite the mother of the family next door to come talk with me. She'll be here this afternoon once Doris leaves.

"Doris, can you pour me some tea?"

She supplies me with my book and a few letters I need to read and respond to. Kay Dooley is coming later to help with my correspondence. I am almost finished with my reading when Ray the mailman arrives. Since he is in early, I ask Doris to make coffee. Ray is such a sweetheart; he calls me "Ma". I first asked him to come in after he saved one of our cats from the Currier's boxer, Felix, that lives two houses down the street. Ray seems to get along with every dog in the neighborhood. As he sits on the chair recently vacated by Doris, the cats greet him individually with a rub or a wave of their tail. He adjusts his ever-present sunglasses, his scars sneaking out for a moment from underneath the rims. "What's wrong with Doris?" he whispers. "She's getting a divorce from Al. He's cheating," I explain. "Well, keep reminding her that I am happily married," he says with a serious tone. I wink as Doris returns.

As she whimpers, divulging her suffering to Ray, I see Bob, the Loutit laundryman, on a course past the stump and around the pool. "Doris, can you get a folding chair for Bob?" The task is interrupted as she pauses to blow her nose. Ray tells me about his ten year old daughter's activities. Bob is ushered into the folding chair and served a cup of coffee by Doris. I greet him, and speak of my dream on Bournemouth Beach, viewing the Isle of Wight. I omit the splints. Ray takes off his cap and brushes his hand backwards through his hair. As he puts the hat back on, he turns to Bob, "When were you in England?" "June, 1944," Bob replies. Straightening in his chair, Ray exclaims, "D Day!" His sunglasses are unable to mask his excitement. Yet, neither follows this exchange with a single word. I've seen this happen before with WWII vets; they nurse their real wounds invisibly, inside. Their conversation ended, they retreated to their chairs to sip their coffee.

After moving on to safer topics, Ray and Bob eventually leave me with my letters and Doris. She is preparing dinner. Using the leftover meatloaf from Sunday, she makes TV dinners by plopping clumps of it in the large section of aluminum plates. After opening and heating canned peas and whipping some instant potatoes, she spoons each of them into the two smaller sections. She covers her imitations with aluminum foil and places them in the freezer. Kay Dooley is here. Her wonderful smile and sharp blue eyes draw my gaze to the door immediately. Though she is even shorter and stouter than Doris, her presence is so much more uplifting. She is the favorite teacher of all the third grade children at Wilson school. She seats herself at the small desk and gently guides the writing leaf down. I dictate to her a letter for our landlord:

Dear Mr. Ray,

I am absolutely heartbroken to discover that your beautiful wife, Susan, is afflicted with Multiple Sclerosis. When the human body weakens the spirit strengthens. You will find with fervent resolve and faith in God that this challenge will imbue your love with an opportunity for compassion and you must retain the belief in the goodness of life. The demands of infirmity, I know all so well, cannot be easily met alone. If I can ever be...

My thoughts come to a stop as I remember the time. The kids will be home momentarily for lunch, and I must discuss it with Doris. I glance at the desk, "Kay, would you like a meal or tea, maybe a cup of coffee?" Kay politely declines, and asks if I would like to continue.

...a source of consolation, please call me. We understand your desire to sell the house is due primarily to the anticipated cost associated with Susan's recent illness. I am happy to inform you that although Bernard and I have been declined in our request for a mortgage, my mother has agreed to pay for the house. She remains quite concerned for my well-being as she understands that a move to another home would be an arduous task due to my paralysis.

She believes your asking price of $7500.00 is beyond her immediate capacity. She has indicated that should you agree to $6000.00, she would pay in cash.

"Kay, can you tidy it up and bring it to a conclusion with another mention of my empathy for Susan?"

After Kay leaves, the house becomes quiet. I stare out at the street as the afternoon sun brightly illuminates the red duplex across from us, transforming each of its windows into a blazing star. When I return my gaze to the room, spots confront my vision. Pockets of growing noise enter the air; the children are coming home. Bernie's bicycle is in view, his baseball glove is dangling from his handlebar as he glides through the gate. He's happy, it seems that he has been all of his young life. His only objections are with his glasses, short hair cuts, and Sister Mary Edgar. Most of these are revealed through jokes. It won't be long before all of his friends flood the house. Joe Regan, Ken Dooley, Billy Nelson, and Bobby Currier are coming over today. All of them are delightful, except for Billy. Neither Bernard nor I like him because he is manipulative and destined for trouble.

Twenty minutes or so pass before Michael steers his Vespa 150 Motor Scooter into the yard. He sets foot in the house without saying hello, changes his clothes, and leaves. This is his ritual of late, our home is merely a hindrance between the time he is able to spend with Phyllis at her house. Whether he is angry or simply unhappy, I'm not sure. Perhaps he is sexually frustrated, like most 17 year old boys.

Music falls down the stairs garishly. I hate the song they are playing, *Mustang Sally*. To write a song about a car seems so silly. Michael never has any patience for their music. I hope soon that they will sing, *And I Love Her*, by the Beatles. It's quite pretty. I will request it over the loudspeaker, once they have finished with the stupid car tune.

Patrick gingerly opens the gate, his blonde hair shimmering in the light. I often tear up at the sight of him, especially when thinking of the abandonment he endured. He is so self-contained, neat, and quiet. He needs no one, not even me. He does not touch me when I tell him how much I love him; he replies, "I know, Ma, you told me yesterday," in a laughing tone. I wonder if painting his side of his room made him happy.

The last one home is David, trailing in. He scans the ground in front of him, leaving the gate open. He limps as speedily as he can inside, and halts at the foot rest at the bottom of my bed. He pours out the contents of his day, a cruel one, with teasing and embarrassment. Steve Burkhart called him "Dako Polio." "What can I do?" I ask him. "Bernie has already done it," he offers. David had told Bernie at recess, who subsequently found Steve's older brother, Joseph. With the bully in tow, Joseph made Steve deliver an apology. I'm uncertain of Bernie's methods at times like these. He and Michael are very protective of David, and their previous means of coercion have landed them in the office of Monsignor Lennon at St. Margaret's School. David affectionately reaches for my hand and flashes me a gentle smile as he hops up to prepare himself some tea.

The music stops, and I ask David to turn on the intercom. "And I Love Her!" I yell into the speaker. The opening bass line is played in unison by two guitars, and another adds a sweet rhythm. Bernie's band has only guitars and a singer. They moved from his room to the stairway so that I might hear them better. "I give her all my love..." Bobby and Bernie are singing. The music moves me to accompany them, but I can't sustain a note. I am at once thrilled by the sound and bitterly disappointed that I cannot be a part of it. Doris pours me a scotch on the rocks. The smooth aroma is stimulating and I close my eyes. Tears form hastily and my chest feels heavy. There is joy in the sadness, excitement occurs simply from feeling. Emotions are my only movement now--they dance inside, billowing fantastically like the wind. I am crying, and it reminds me of the endless, angry despair I felt in the hospital. I am consumed by a longing to touch and to be touched back, to love and to be loved back. Michael hates me, Patrick has no real feelings one way or another, at least David needs me. Bernie loves me, but it is easy because we are so alike. Yet, when he rubs my feet and kisses me goodbye each morning, I know his heart is in the right place. I think of Bernard last--his love is the most complex. He touches me out of my need, but not his. Sometimes, at night, he joins me on the rocking bed, holding my hand and whispering to me. I can only move my right index finger stiffly. It is all that God has left me with, my finger to tap on Bernard's palm. The smoothness of his hand under my rigid touch feels electric and kindles a feeling as ardent as a deep, warm kiss. It seems so cruelly poetic that passion's expression could be limited to such a small gesture.

"Like a Rolling Stone!" I insist into the intercom. I can see Bobby's face light up; I know that this selection will make him happy, as it gives him a chance to exhibit his extensive memory for lyrics. His emulation sounds like Bob Dylan, though I doubt that he, or any of the other boys with maybe the exception of Billy, knows what the words really mean. Bobby belts out "didn't you," with feeling.

Doris is crying at the kitchen table, her hands covering her face. Tears drip steadily onto the surface with the consistency of an intravenous bag. She catches me looking at her in the mirror. "Go on home, Honey, I mouth in the reflection. She mouths back, "Thank you."

Bernard is coming home early; he has to be at Church for a Benediction. He breezes in and kisses me softly. He is chipper and talkative, and the resentment that I had been feeling all day dissolves in his effervescence. I'm reminded of his frequent comment, "I like playing an instrument--when it's in tune." Our conversation has a pleasant harmony. Beyond us, the children are happily eating their dinners and discussing their plans to go outside soon for *Capture the Flag.* Michael is absent, eating at the Gentile's house again. When Bernard begins to feed me, he talks about his morbidly deemed boss, "Rigor Mortis", and I realize in the middle of his story that I do not know the man's real name. I know that there has been an issue over Bernard's chronic tardiness, but he can't leave the house for work until Doris arrives, and lately her punctuality has been as unpredictable as her mood. The children run out to play and Bernard goes to Church as the woman from next door, Pat Kralik, arrives. "You wanted to see me?" she asks shyly. I can see that she is in her twenties although she already has three children. Her husband, Joe Kralik, is a gambler and drinker. As if he were in character, he wears a white tee shirt and often has a Pall Mall filter-less cigarette dangling out of the side of his mouth. I don't know how they met, but he should count his lucky stars.

No sooner has Pat Kralik left after my proposal when Michael comes in. He slams down his application for Allegheny College. "Are you happy NOW?" he asks angrily. He leaves as abruptly as he arrived leaving me stunned. I contemplate his question and oddly I feel happy. Not because Michael has completed the forms after much badgering on my part, but because I am excited about this young woman. Am I happy that Michael hates living here? Does it give me joy that he has stopped helping and seems to resent the possibility that I am happy? No, because I am obliged to encourage his education. Allegheny College is inexpensive and a simple arrangement has already been made with Grandma Mulligan for a place for him to stay. Yet, I can almost understand his anxiety about leaving Phyllis--young love has so much faith in itself.

Bernard comes home after Benediction and his subsequent obligatory appearance at The Hitching Post. I know the sound of his car and I wait for him to appear in the mirror as he opens the side door. His eyes meet mine in the mirror and I am instantly relieved. When he is drunk, he hides the evidence with his gaze cast down, averting me. He comes in close to kiss me and asks how the interview went. "You'll be training her on Saturday. She is young, friendly, and attractive, and she lives right next door." I tell him about Michael and he laughs and asks me, "ARE you happy now?" Later, as he puts the application in an envelope, stamps it, and places it on the kitchen table he looks at me in the mirror and says: "How about NOW?" "Not yet," I reply. I chuckle but I am reluctant to join in this banter because of our vulnerability to each other's words. The discussion of happiness seems to me to be the most frightening prospect imaginable. I wake up every day and fill it with as many people, appointments, and activities as I possibly can in order to avoid the contemplation of happiness. I have a sad feeling that alcohol does the same for Bernard.

He and I go over the scheduling for the next few days, and

conduct interviews with David, Patrick, and Bernie individually. We plan homework and other routines for Boy Scouts, Little League, and Altar Boys, and we pay them their allowances. Penny is on my lap again, cleaning herself with her back leg straight up in the air. She looks up at me with her crossed eyes, then resumes her grooming. Penny is the only cat that is not afraid of the rocking bed. She waits for the foot of the bed to be closest to the floor and hops on, walking with supreme confidence and purpose as the pendulum motion of the bed lifts and lowers her.

Bernard takes his time putting me to bed and we talk about music, Michael, and Pat Kralik. Once I am rocking he kisses me goodnight and goes to his room to read. I close my eyes and think of tomorrow. I feel Penny finding her way to my lap. "Am I happy NOW?" is stuck in my head like that horrible tune, *Hang on Sloopy*, that wedges into my sub-conscious once in a while. Bernard will be the one to talk to him about the importance of school and our sacrifice for him, but Michael only views his father as the enforcer of my scheming. For now, I am drifting off to the sands of Bournemouth Beach and the chance to walk, to scratch an itch, and to blow my own nose.

In my dream I drive the bus from Bournemouth to the Cliffs of Dover. As I shift the gears I look in the mirror and there's my reflection, I am in the bed, in the bus and in paralysis. I turn away and stare straight ahead at the road. I want this dream to give me movement, but it only offers fear and apprehension instead. I want to walk. I want to touch. Emotions are my only movement now—they dance inside, fantastically, like the wind.

Chapter Nineteen - Dad's Lecture

Carnegie Institute

ON THE SUMMIT OF BEACON HILL
PINCKNEY AND ANDERSON STREETS
BOSTON MASSACHUSETTS 02114

May 24, 1965

Bernard J. Mulligan, Sc. M.
Chief, Bacteriologist
Veterans Administration Hospital
Providence 8, Rhode Island

Dear Bernie:

Please find enclosed a list of the topics that we would like for you to lecture on at Carnegie.

The amount of material to be covered will probably necessitate the preparation of two or three lectures.

The topics have been scheduled for the week of May 31st; preferably June 3rd. and 4th. Please let us know whether or not the subjects and/or the time are convenient for you.

Sincerely,

Bill

William T. Barnes
Technical Director

WTB/jmc

P. S. You may have as much time as you like.

Tested Training for the Allied Medical Professions

Dad's Invitation from the Carnegie Institute

In 1965, Bernard was anticipating the death of his father, who was severely afflicted with prostate cancer. He had flown to see him on May 23rd. However, he was scheduled to present a lecture on June 3rd, so he could not stay long. He described the trip in detail in his diary:

"Left Rumford about 8:15 on a smooth, but slow, ride to Boston. I got right on the plane, which doesn't look very big right now. I will probably have a parking ticket for my car when I get back. I am now looking at a dingy, smoky wing, and exhaust on the left side. Could do with a great big shot! Inside it looks like a cramped Pullman Coach. I am not calm and my hands are cold, but here I am. They just started the motor which vibrates the whole caboodle. I must be out of my mind."

Bernard was picked up in Buffalo by his nephew, Jim, in a '57 Chevy Sedan. After a bumpy landing, a frenetic ride down Route 19 from Erie to Meadville followed.

"Jim met me at the airport and drove me to Meadville. I was more nervous in his car than in the plane. Came straight to Arch Street where Sister James Francis and Mom were surprised. Sister ran right away to give Dad the news and with a big lie about my having to go to Buffalo and decided to come over here as long as I was close. Dad told her that it was the best news he had had and seems to have perked him up. Right now I am sitting by his side."

"I wonder if my Dad will last until July," Bernard pondered in his writing. His father had once possessed a physical strength that was legendary, from carrying bathtubs, pipes, and tools up three flights of stairs. It was difficult for the family to accept the loss of such a strong figure. *"It is too much to see him now and to remember him standing on the banks of French Creek ready to dive in…without apparel."*

Despite the sad circumstances, Bernard was surprised by how

good he felt. He explained that *"aside from my father's condition, the visit was quite enjoyable."* His exuberance over a simple meal of *"fried chicken, creamed potatoes and beets,"* attests to the deprivation of peace and normal human discourse he endured at home. *"I met more of my old friends than ever before in a short amount of time,"* he also noted. The simple yet comforting pleasure of leisurely meals and good company pleased him greatly. The gift of reflection and quiet as he sauntered the streets in Meadville, and the absolute luxury of introspection mixed with his grief.

His visit felt far too brief, but his lecture neared, and he needed to return to Rhode Island to collect his materials. On the day of his engagement at Carnegie, his intention was to leave early and stop for breakfast at Paul's Diner. This neighborhood favorite catered to many of the congregation as it was next to St. Margaret's Church. He thought he could go for an English muffin while he reviewed his notes for the lecture. Woefully, his plan was foiled by chores and annoyances at home. He also needed to stop in at the hospital before going to the Institute.

Bernard knew that he needed to focus on the lecture, but his thoughts were scattered. He was mulling over the recent past. Two weeks ago, he had taken my mother's bus with the rocking bed and generator to Boston to pick up Meme. As he drove towards Boston again, the crowding of events, responsibilities, and nonsense free associated with his attempts at concentration. He and Marie had gone over the lecture many times and he was prepared, and this is what he was working on in the bacteriology lab every workday. However, when the time came for his presentation and he stood before the blackboard, he gazed at the students blankly. He stumbled with his introduction and grasped for the right pace and tone. He soon recovered, though, and found his voice so clear and strong that everyone sat in rapt attention. It was an engaging lecture, filled with facts, interaction, and humor. The agility of his mind, momentarily freed from the confines of sacrifice and duty, brightened his green eyes and gave him confidence.

As he drove home he initially reveled in his success. Like his time in Meadville, this experience of conducting a successful lecture invigorated him, but it also left him dejected. He could see what his life could have been. As he drove his car across the Massachusetts border into Pawtucket, Rhode Island, his mood continued to darken. He pondered his own death and the significance of his life. He parked his car in front of *The Hitching Post* and pushed his way through the door. The bartender brought him a beer and a shot, and Bernard took them to an empty table. He looked out the window and cried silently, mourning the loss of his father and bereaving the diminished prospect of a happy life.

Chapter Twenty - Michael at Allegheny College

Allegheny College

In November of 1966, Michael and I drove 600 miles to Meadville together, to begin his studies at Allegheny College. I was invited along to provide company, and I would return by bus. He had a 1955 Chevy with a three speed transmission on the column. Tears hid in the corners of his eyes as he drove. I knew that he missed Phyllis, but I stared out the window at the snow-crusted countryside, pretending to be unaware of his crying. We seldom spent time alone together, and being in the car with him gave us an opportunity to relate. He lectured me about drugs and which friends of mine he didn't like. He controlled the radio. Eventually, the conversation loosened and we laughed and joked. At one point, Michael mimed the slow deliberate raising of a pipe. He rested the tip of the imaginary pipe on his lower lip thoughtfully before looking out his window at a passing motorist. Pulling the pipe down, he rasped out of the side of his mouth, "Jackass!" Neither of us could stop laughing at his impression of Dad.

We stayed at a motel in Syracuse overnight and I slept on the couch. The next morning, we had a large breakfast and got an early start. Michael realized in Batavia that he had left his suitcase in the motel room. Michael's mood worsened. "One hundred and fifty miles wasted," he muttered, after retrieving it. His thoughts returned to negativity about the move. Michael was going to be living at Grandma Mulligan's house, whose presence he did not enjoy.

During a previous summer in Meadville, Michael and I had snuck off with our pretty third cousin, Mary Theresa, to see Elvis Presley's new movie, *Roustabout.* After we purchased our tickets, Michael told me to get lost and meet him and Mary Theresa by the marquee after the movie ended. I sat six or seven rows behind them as the "Coming Attractions" rolled. I knew Michael had no intentions for Mary Theresa, but he relished the idea of appearing as if he was with a good-looking young woman on a date. The theater darkened, and Elvis Presley, in his sublime coolness, dominated the screen. The theater was packed with teenagers quietly staring at the cinematic giant. A motorcycle expertly revved by our hero skidded to a stop; the rear wheel squared the bike horizontally on the screen. Elvis vaulted from the seat of the motorcycle and began to sing when suddenly, off to the right in the aisle, a piercing voice cut through the darkness. "Michael and Mary Theresa! Come here this minute!". They jumped from their seats and ran toward our Grandmother's stern figure. They followed her out of the movie in utter humiliation. I knew Michael would be angry. Mary Theresa had forgotten to get permission from her mother, our Aunt Gly, about her excursion. Gly complained to Grandma, and she determinedly set out to retrieve us. I snuck out and joined them on the sidewalk in front of the theater. Michael's ears glowed red as he interrupted Gly and Grandma's ensuing lecture. "You are not my boss!" he hissed. We all walked back to Arch Street quietly, accompanied only by the quiet sobbing of Mary Theresa.

Now, Michael was expected to live happily at Arch Street with our grandmother. Under duress, his behavior was uncharacteristically bad. He came in late, skipped classes, and insulted my grandmother with insolence and sulking. This must have come as a shock to Grandma, because my father had written to her earlier in the year:

"Michael is my right hand and I am hoping I will lose him to Allegheny College. So you know I don't have much sense. Anyway I hope if I get him to Allegheny you could give him house room at 415. He is very good company and very mature as you can imagine with what he does for our very unusual home."

Michael had been in Meadville a mere month when he wrote a nasty letter to my parents. The content of his letter stirred my father to anger. My Dad wrote back:

Dear Mike,

We received your long and interesting letter and I admit that I have been remiss in writing to you. I would appreciate if you would get off this "anti-people" kick or is it an "anti-relative" binge? Your gun case is on its way and enclosed is the check for 15.00.

There can be no question about how much I love and admire you. You will need to sit down and quietly think about the times Mummy and I have staunchly worked for you. Your jealous remarks about Bernie are not reasonable. Your taunting of your mother with selfishness is very unkind and not in line with the character that you have usually exhibited over the years. It may be true that we have not given you as much vocal praise as you deserve and need but we will try to do so in future. Take care of yourself. Will be glad to see you at Christmas. We are turning the house upside down to find the bank book.

Your loving father,

B.J.Mulligan

P.S.
Give my love to Grandma.

Michael did not attend a second semester at Allegheny College. My parents were disappointed, and upon his return it was clear that there was tension, although it eventually diffused into the flux of each new day. Michael received a draft notice. Somehow in our harried states, we had all forgotten that he no longer had a deferment to spare him. We were stunned at the thought of him in Vietnam, fighting a war.

Chapter Twenty-One - Exercising My Bad Judgement

Dad's Workplace

I came down the stairs on a spring morning in 1967 to a commotion in my mother's room. Pat Kralik had come over, as she did every day, but my mother was still rocking in her bed. By this time on any other morning, my father would have set her up. As my mother's face came into view, I could see a panicked expression that cemented the seriousness of the situation. As her face descended, pulled down by the rocking bed, I asked what was wrong. Pat looked at me squarely and said, "Your father did not come home last night." I knew at once that I would not be attending school this day. This event was without precedent. Dad always came home. He was our foundation, the caretaker, and the reason we could all pretend that the lives we were living were normal. I stopped my mother's bed and fitted her with the chest-piece. As I picked up the hose to insert it in the round hole of the shell, I patted her hand and promised her that it would be all right. She glanced at me briefly and quickly averted eye contact. She stared furtively out the window. "I daresay, it is my fault," she sighed. "I really let him have it last night."

We called the hospitals and police stations, to no avail. The bars were closed. It was too cold in the parks and we checked the bus. We called the Gentile's house and Florence told my mother that she would send Phillip Sr. over when he returned from work to help with the search. All the while my mother stared out the window silently. She did not cry, and all offers of food, tea, or scotch were politely declined. Emergencies had developed into a familiar way of life; we all shifted to automatic pilot. Pat prepared meals and transported the children to and from school. She also explained the crisis to the flow of people who came to our door. Within a few hours, ten people were driving the streets and searching for his car. Mr. Gentile arrived around three, and beckoned me and Michael to join him.

We drove across the red bridge and through the East Side on our way to downtown Providence. It appeared to me that he had a plan, and I asked where we were going. "You know, Bernie, your father's life is pretty tough. We all look up to him," he said. He chose his words carefully. "Your Dad has enormous responsibilities." I am not sure what I replied with, but I knew that I could not imagine our lives without Dad functioning on at least one cylinder. Mr. Gentile wanted to know if I knew my way around the VA Hospital where my Dad worked. My father and I had collaborated on a science project that required placing agar jars around the house, exposing them to the odious micro-organisms that populated the corners of each room and collecting them. We then went for two weeks at night and watched the life flourish in his lab. I knew the place well.

We pulled into the lot in front of the big brick building; it looked like a huge Monopoly hotel piece flanked by two houses. I led the way, past the nurses' station and administration, to an empty stairwell near the maintenance department. Dad and I had chosen this route before to avoid interaction with co-workers and patients. We eventually arrived at the lab on the sixth floor. It was very quiet. As we walked slowly and stealthily past the empty desks we could hear the faint sound of snoring. Following that sound, we found him on an examination table.The table was covered with a white sheet of paper. "Bernie?" Mr. Gentile queried. My Dad woke up, his hand reaching to a grey deposit of two days hair growth on his face. "Oh, hi, Phillip," was his raspy reply. "Dad, what are you doing?" I asked, my relief mingled with confusion. He sat up and stretched. His clothes were wrinkled and disheveled. "I am exercising my bad judgment," he answered, meeting my eyes head on. He looked over to Mr. Gentile and asked him to assure my mother that he'd be home the following night. He did return home, as he said he would. For the next few days, there were many conferences behind the closed doors of my mother's room.

Our home returned to normal, except that we were no longer allowed to play loud guitar in the house. It didn't matter to me. The *Ultimates* had dismantled, because I kept bringing in songs like *Rain* by the Beatles and *Love is All Around* by The Troggs. My bandmates made it clear that they didn't want to play those songs as it would be difficult for the audience to dance to the music. With no place to practice the band disintegrated. I retreated to my room and played my acoustic 12 string, immersed in lugubrious ballads and psychedelia.

Chapter Twenty-Two - Dad

Strange that though life always ends the same the story could be so wildly unique for each of us.

From 1965 to 1967, much had changed for me. I quit Boy Scouts, Little League, and my role as an Altar Boy. Dad had been the coach for Fram's baseball team for two years, my Little League team, and he had been assistant scoutmaster. He dropped those responsibilities soon after I left each organization. We still drove to Church together on Sunday. We played Scrabble and card games in the evening with my mother and anyone else who was around. We were all flabbergasted by his skill at Scrabble. Once he scored over 75 points with the word, 'cyst'. More often than not, he would place words down that were drawn from his world of microbiology and bacteriology, but he also knew the board and would take advantage of triple word and letter scores. His sense of humor was beginning to make sense to me as I approached the age of fifteen. He enjoyed wordplay, particularly with common sayings and proverbs. "Don't spite the nose that feeds you," he'd say, or, "If a tree falls in the forest are there two birds in the bush?" This fracturing of well-known phrases particularly irritated my mother. "Oh, Bernard!" she'd whisper almost to herself. His understanding and appreciation for the English language made him a formidable conversationalist. He told me that adverbs were the most exciting parts of speech, because they described action while adjectives only described persons, places, and things. He warned me about the adverb "frankly." "If someone starts a sentence with this adverb, you should hold onto your wallet," he'd say.

He tried to teach me piano. I only wanted to learn chords so that I could play piano while my friends played guitar. One night, while Bill Barnes was our dinner guest, they began playing gospel and religious songs. The piano was in his room, but my mother would listen as the music would resonate down the hall and she would make requests. "Bernie, certainly you could accompany them with your guitar?" she urged. I always tuned my guitar to the piano, as it was concert pitch, so I pulled my 12 string Gibson out and listened to them play. I found that the chords were pretty intuitive and I knew all of the songs. I brought my guitar into his room, strapped, so that it rested in front of me. Soon we were jamming away, and the best tune by far that we played was 'My Lord What a Morning.' My father was making up the words and urging Bill and me to do the same. "You can hear the drain gurgling, you can hear the drain gurgling, you can hear the drain gurgling when the stars begin to fall," he sang. We dissolved frequently into laughter as the verses became more absurd. My father and Bill played with raucous abandon when they got excited by the music. When it was over and we reconvened in my mother's room, Dad made no comment about my playing. However, the following Sunday he told me to listen closely to the Introductory portion of the Mass. As I ambled piously down the aisle between the rows of pews, St. Margaret's huge sonorous pipe organ emitted its usual minor-key-driven, lugubrious music. This time, however, I recognized the song, although it had been slowed considerably. My father was playing, "We Can Work It Out," a Beatles tune he had learned to play after he had pilfered the song from my pile of sheet music. I construed his behavior as a validation, but he may also have been trying to tell me how primitive my music was. I know I caused him angst as he stated in his diary.

There was plenty of interaction between my father and me. We talked about baseball, school, and what was wrong with the car, but we did not discuss his father's death. In my teenage mind, my father was like any other institution that I confronted daily. School, paper route, my band, Michael, and most significantly, my mother, dominated my life. My father and I discussed the Holy Catholic Church, the Mass and Confession. We had a very animated and prolonged discussion about Confession.

As we drove slowly down Ruth Avenue on our way to St. Margaret's Church, he unexpectedly turned to the curb and parked the car. "Dad we're gonna be late," I said. He looked at me and I could see cars passing by behind his head out the driver window. I think he enjoyed the thought of my having to grapple with the sin concerning lateness to the Sunday Obligation. "I talked to Father Anthony," he ventured, taking his pipe out of his mouth. I said nothing, paralyzed. "He says you want to know what commandment is broken when someone smokes grass." "Dad!" I exclaimed in horror, "confession is private! If a Priest commits a Mortal Sin…I mean, can he actually… isn't it…" He pointed the stem of his pipe an inch from my humiliated face. "Do you smoke grass?" He asked menacingly. "I won't ever again," I replied. He nodded his head, put the car in gear and clenched his pipe, which began to billow like a locomotive. I turned the radio to WPRO. "Father Anthony! Confession!" I pondered. I was outraged by their collusion. My Dad scrawled in his diary: *"Bernie turned in sick tonight. He has been a morose and self-centered problem of late."*

To better understand my father, one would need to attend two Funerals, two Benedictions, five Masses, and one Marriage every week for ten years. One would have to hold his lover every day and night, only to feel dead weight in return. One would have to be immersed in a world of chaos and nonsense. He expressed the unhappiness about the difficulties in his home in his diary because he could not express it to the ones he loved:

"So much is going on constantly, it is hard to write it all down. The weekend had really been a bad dream with the teenagers – it is too cumulative, and the mixture of boys and girls produces undercurrents of love, hate, jealousy, and loneliness. Also, there is callousness and ignorance and bad manners inside, even when outwardly the manners are good. The incessant pounding of the records they play excites them to frustrated, juvenile, and non-comprehending sexual expression. They are as addicted to cigarettes as I am to alcohol. I am in the certified doghouse with Marie because I didn't show enthusiastic appreciation for her when I got home on Tuesday night. I didn't acknowledge somehow how much she was doing for me, and she dropped a bomb about our lack of sex life. While doing Marie up and turning her, I got a good talking to about the way I muddle things up; no planning, try to do things during lunch time or other impossible times, etc, etc. All perfectly true. The three areas of my life are as untidy and as far behind as possible. Home, lab, and church. Tough day at the office. I got the national survey out and only to receive another from Boston. Late in the day, Mr. Smith cornered me about drinking. I knew this was coming sooner or later, and I hope that I can face into the wind and the terrible sickness of

withdrawal without help. Drinking is the cause of problems at home and work; I must win, because too many people will go down with my defeat. I feel exhausted, and when one issue diminishes, another seems to fill its place instantly. For example, it became very cold during the night. Raw and bitter; of course, then, we ran out of oil. I blew out the main fuses trying to warm up with the stove and electric fire. Marie's bed had to be frantically hand-cranked. The only plug working was by my bed. Finally, Marie was set up with a big extension cord from my plug to her respirator. It seems strange that though life always ends the same, that story could be so wildly unique for each us, forced to read our tale to the end. If it weren't for this diary I could scarcely remember how I got to this place, running around like a chicken without a head. It is no good talking or thinking about writing a diary. It must be written. It requires unusual self discipline and self interest. It seems to be the only self-interest I am allowed to have, at times."

As he opened the large wooden doors to St. Margaret's Church, he passed the off-white porcelain holy water fonts on either side of the inner doorway. He turned left towards the darkened spiral staircase that led up to the choir loft. The stairs were so tight that one had to wait for the descending party to complete their descent before heading up. It was September 24, and the bright fall sun exploded through the stained glass windows, fragmenting in colored beams across the floor. As he reached the top of the stairs, he looked over the railing at the pews and the carpeted aisle below that led to the large Altar. Under the immense stained glass window at the front, Jesus was depicted with a gold crown blending into a blue aura. The whole Church was drenched in light. Dad felt sad. It had been 10 years this month that his life had changed irrevocably. He wondered if persevering was the same as living.

With shaking hands, he grasped the instructions for the hastily planned funeral. Elizabeth Scanlon, dead at only 9 years of age, was being laid to rest. Her forty-five classmates from Saint Margaret's School quietly stood in line down the main stairs of the Church. Women were weeping and gasping, their handkerchiefs unable to keep up. Men stood solemnly in shirts and ties, heads bowed, with their hands forming a chevron near their belt. September's sun and clear dry air pierced the opened doors in strange contrast to the murky confusion and loss felt in the Church. Bernard put the funeral instructions on his bench. He quickly realized that he was going to be required to sing. This was a High Mass according to the sheet. He had written in his diary about the funeral:

"On Tuesday, there was a funeral for a little girl who had been one of David's classmates. I did all right until the Agnus Dei, when my voice just broke up, and I had great difficulty singing the rest of the Mass. What precipitated or catalyzed this was one of the school girls passing out under the seat with great unconscious wailing--it frightened three other little girls so much that they wouldn't return to the same bench. They had been frightened out into the middle aisle."

Chapter Twenty-Three - 1968

Dad with Meadville Reporter Paul Brown

The cumulative effect of events like the assassinations of Martin Luther King, Jr. and Robert Kennedy, the Tet Offensive in Vietnam, demonstrations against the Establishment, and the provocative ramblings of Spiro Agnew infused the population with fear in 1968. The turmoil shaped the music, literature, and films of the time. Fashion changed dramatically. Suddenly, everyone wanted to make their own personal expression, defying the tranquil conformity of the previous generation. The repertoire of hats, bags, and glasses expanded. Bold colors splashed across album covers and movie screens. Reviewers of this history have been so captured by the bright colors and playful slang of the time that their retrospectives tend to obfuscate the seriousness of the clash between youth and the government. The consequences of political subversion were tangible and harsh. Many jailed for refusing the draft or forced to flee to Canada could attest to the real commitment made for convictions against the prevailing order. Angry fingers were being pointed. Apathy was impossible under the condition that everyone knew someone fighting, injured, killed in, protesting, or trying to escape the war. My father wanted the chaos to stop and he stood on the side of Nixon and Agnew. One of the doctors at the VA Hospital had been murdered in the parking lot for drug money. This incident helped Nixon's "law and order" position resonate with Dad. My mother loved the emerging counter culture, its music, and wild ideas. Her rocking bed sheets became flowery and ablaze with color. She listened to Leonard Cohen and avidly read the lyrics. So while my friends and I shot rubber sticking darts at the 11 inch black and white television screen in my room whenever Nixon, Johnson, General Westmoreland, or John Wayne appeared on the screen, she immersed herself in the artistic expression that was being generated. When the TV reported on the bombing of Hanoi, she empathized with the recipients of the carnage. It stimulated the memory of her distress during the Battle of Britain. "Frightful!" she'd exclaim. "You don't even know."

That summer, Patrick had painted flowers on the front of the bus above the windshield. My father drove the bus to Pennsylvania in August. Dad was perfectly sober throughout that summer and fall.

The effort that it took to reach that state had been more difficult than anyone, except my father, imagined.

My mother had asked me to meet with my father and her behind closed doors. My father sat in the easy chair, pipe billowing, as my mother outlined the issue and the proposed solution. Dad interrupted the discussion to announce that it was something he had been thinking about for quite some time. In his diary, he described the tension at work as his superior had brought his drinking up during a review. His entry into rehabilitation was a collaborative effort between home and work. He would be in for a couple of weeks. My mother continued telling me that I would be driving Dad to the VA for his admission and that I would need to be at home every night. I would be his sole visitor during his stay. I would pick him up when his treatment was complete. We would be very quiet about the situation.

Admission day arrived, and we got into my 1959 VW Bug. I tried to survey my father's expression, but he stared at the ground on the way to the car, and once in the car, he stared out the passenger window. "Do you want the sunroof opened," I asked quietly. There was no response. Once in the parking lot, I took the keys from the ignition and my father grasped my forearm. "I am so sorry," he quavered. I said nothing.

He stayed for a month, and the first week was agonizing. He did not recognize me when I came into his room. I wondered if any of his co-workers visited and witnessed his torturous bout with delirium tremens. Each night I came home and reported his progress to my mother. I did not divulge what I was actually seeing until the second week, when he suddenly showed rapid improvement. We played chess and listened to Red Sox games during these visits. I kept telling him that we missed him, and that Pat Kralik and I were doing well with his responsibilities, and that mom was strong. Taking on his workload was a revelation to me, and I felt that I understood him that much more from finding my way through the routine that had ground him down year after year.

After six weeks he was discharged. As we left the hospital

together, he walked straight and quickly to his car. The effects of alcohol had become so subtly ingrained in his movements over time that the purposefulness in his stride was new and unusual to me. He radiated vigor and determination. I had driven his Buick station wagon to pick him up, at his insistence. He slid into the driver's seat and clicked the ignition on with an enthusiasm I had not seen in a while. "Well, Dad, are you going to be alright?" I asked. "I'm fine," he replied, as he drove the familiar streets past downtown. He took his pipe out and banged the spent ashes into the ashtray. "Bernie, I can't cure polio!" he stated emphatically. "That's a fact."

Chapter Twenty-Four - Points of View

My parents' worry about Michael's involvement in the war complicated their ability to reach consensus on politics. My father acknowledged that my mother's perception had been irrevocably affected by her firsthand experience of war's devastation. Coming up from the bomb shelter, she had seen the litter of debris from torn buildings and body parts. He once called her naïve, because she believed the peaceful sentiments of the songs being played by her children. With a flash of her eyes, he quickly rephrased the "naïve" part of his argument. Their discussions were generally civil and one would not interrupt the other. Michael's commitment had increased from two years as a draftee to four years as a result of his entrance into officer training. My parents had encouraged this strategy, hoping that the war would end by the time he finished school, as well as understanding that while most draftees became infantrymen, Mike's intelligence would likely land him a safer position in the army. I chose not to engage my father in political discussions, but it was clear that I was against the war.

On March 4th 1969, my parents, along with Patrick and David loaded the bus to embark upon a journey to Fort Belvoir, Virginia to attend Michael's graduation from Officer's Candidate School. Michael was now a Second Lieutenant, and my mother and father were giddy with pride. The trip to Fort Belvoir was arduous and problematic. The bus developed mechanical problems and traffic was heavy. Patrick had learned mechanical skills and was quite helpful. Dad depended on Patrick who seemed to enjoy the challenge. David and Patrick were keenly aware of Dad's sobriety by this time. My father wrote in his diary: "The boys went into the restaurant which turned out to be a beer joint full of revelers. They said that they were glad that Dad didn't go in because of his problem."

***

Marie watched cars shimmering in the heat as she was carried along Route 95. Each face that passed them on the road or through the many parallel toll lanes had a bright yet flat character, like a slide in a View-Master toy. She had grown accustomed to the more prolonged gawking that some strangers would indulge in when they stopped. She met each gaze with full eye contact. Bernard sat in the driver's seat, face cast down to the stick shift, his pipe drooping. He glanced at the heat gage and turned to look at his wife nervously. "We'd better stop, dear, the engine needs water." They kept on the highway for the next quarter mile, just to pass the tollbooth. As they drove through, the attendant smiled at Marie as she refused my father's money. Marie's heart swelled; she felt visibly human.

Bernard navigated the bus off the freeway in Lyme, Connecticut. He parked under a huge willow tree at a rest stop. Patrick and David ran out to the picnic tables. A warm breeze animated the willow's branches to dance around her window. The family was alone. The rest area was empty and the trash barrels were spilling over.

"Honey, I am worried sick about Michael. I know what he's accomplished is impressive... but what good is it if he dies over there?" Marie's voice broke over the last few words.

"Do you know that he is making as much as I am?" he replied shaking his head. "I miss his rent payments. Now we only get $20.00 a month from Bernie."

"Oh stop it, Bernard! Aren't you concerned at all?"

***

We all attended Michael's ceremony with the Gentile family, who had driven down separately. My mother could not get over how "dashing" Mike looked in his officer's uniform. My father was impressed by his sudden maturity and by his salary. On the drive home they discussed the Vietnam War, and how relieved they were that Mike's first assignment was elsewhere.

In the summer of 1969, facing imminent involuntary induction into the service, I made up my mind to get Michael's advice. I met him on Ruth Avenue when he was home on leave and asked him what I should do. Michael smiled kindly, "Bernie, if you get drafted they will put you in the infantry. If you join, you can choose an MOS, (Military Occupation Specialist) as long as you do well on the aptitude tests." We walked together quietly just as we had when we walked to the bus stop or to the ballfield during the years of our childhood. On Frederick Street he paused. "Take it easy," he said as he veered off to walk towards Phylis's house. "You too," I mumbled as he ambled away. I hiked through the golf course and considered my options—picking a job out of harm's way might not be a bad move. As radical as I was at the time, I was not about to head for Canada or risk going to jail. I sat on the crest of a sand trap. I was watching a robin perched on a bright red ball washer when I heard the thwack of a golf club followed by a scream of frustration.

Chapter Twenty-Five - Bernie As A Soldier

Bernie Mulligan, Basic Training

I stared at the strips of insulation protruding out of the cardboard that held it in place, comprising my bedroom ceiling. The lyrics and tune of "Golden Slumbers" from *Abbey Road* floated around my cranium.

Once there was a way to get back homeward
Once there was a way to get back home…

There was no backing out of the army. I skulked down the stairs. I knew that my mother would try to be strong when she greeted me. “I think I made a mistake, Ma.” I said. Tears flowed down her cheeks, wetting her t-shirt collar as it moved under the respirator. She replied unconvincingly, “You are doing the right thing. You’ll see. You are just a little nervous.” I kissed her, picked up my suitcase, and followed my dad out to the car. She and I had listened to "Draft Morning" by the Byrds with Ken Dooley the night before, and she had wept. It had seemed like tears of relief; we had been in denial all summer as the day approached. As the house disappeared from view, I thought about my mom’s words. I wasn’t feeling any better. My father could see that I was upset. “Bernie, we are going to miss you terribly, but within a day or so you’ll feel better. When you get out, the government will pay for your college.” Dad’s words were more helpful. When we got to the AFEES station and parked the car, we were both crying. Any consolation had evaporated and my stomach ached. “You’ll be with men much older than you, but you are tough,” he said firmly. “Remember if you ever need anything…” He wiped his glasses before continuing instinctively, “except money.” I knew he was dead serious, but as we looked out the windshield, we both started to laugh.

My mother started adjusting to the new circumstances before I had even jumped on the bus for my journey to Fort Dix. Patrick and David had already started to pitch in more. Patrick had been taking over the mechanical chores from my father and David began to talk to Mom about poetry and music. “Now, David,” she said, "you will be moving into Bernie’s room and Patrick will stay in the room you have shared. You will need to be more responsible now."

My friends continued to come over and the parade of vendors, postal workers, and neighbors continued unabated into her room, all clamoring for attention. My mother tutored them, and listened empathetically as they discussed the turmoil of boys, other girls, and the constraints of their parents. These teenagers became part of the community that met my mother's physical and emotional needs. Patrick and David's burden was alleviated to a great extent by their presence. The copious number of letters my mother wrote in 1969 are transcribed in their handwriting. They travelled in the bus to Scarborough Beach and Lincoln Woods Lake standing next to my mother, cranking her bed, or feeding her and giving her tea, talking all the while. Instinctively, they would push her glasses up in mid-sentence as my father drove the bus. My mother's hair was being styled and washed frequently, and lipstick was being applied expertly. Everyone called her "Ma."

My father disappeared into the background, appearing only for his obligatory kiss to her as he escaped out the door on his way to work. Yet when he drove the bus, he exploded into character, flipping his fingers like a trumpet in front of his nose at the honking drivers, grinding the transmission of the tired old Reo Bus, "Queenie", and looking in the side view mirror with a grin at the accumulation of cars. Police often would pull the bus over, especially now that it was painted powder blue with dark red and black streaks and flowers. They'd step up the stairs into the bus after walking slowly along the side. The policeman would always have their firm demeanor shattered by the appearance of my mother in the bed, hose sticking out of her chest-piece with the garish colored sheets framing her. Teenagers would flock up around her bed and my father would soak it all in. He'd step outside with the policemen as if to console him, banging the ashes of his pipe in the palm of his hand. More often than not, his license and registration had expired. Fortunately, the police never really got that far into the process, and even if they did, the mountain of logistical issues confronting an arrest or citation deterred them. The police of East Providence knew the bus and its occupants well. They would wave cheerfully as it passed.

When the bus returned from a trip, all the occupants flew into action as my mother was brought out the emergency exit by stretcher and lifted back into her rocking bed. "Ma, where do you want this?" they'd ask, looking at her inquisitively in one of her many mirrors. As dad walked out of the bus, his gait slowed and his hands trembled. He would invariably escape the madness to his room and close the door.

Chapter Twenty-Six - Basic Thanksgiving

Twenty Rounds

At Basic Training all the recruits looked the same. Variations in cadets were essentially limited to height, weight, and orthodontia. Having a shaved head, wearing a uniform, and performing a strict routine each day had a grueling effect on me. It seemed like the homogenous, tedious environment had psychological effects on everyone, although few would probably admit it. Conformity to the group is conducive to following orders and accepting authority. My first day at Fort Dix, New Jersey was October 29th, 1969, and after four weeks I began to observe some personalities beginning to emerge from the platoon. John Machado slept in the bunk next to mine; he seemed good natured. Once, during these early days, he inserted $0.35 into one of the vending machines in the barracks and the machine was unresponsive—no coke and no coin return. Later that day, he stole a clip of twenty rounds for his M-16 from the rifle range. Just before the evening formation, he emptied twenty rounds into the vending machine. The barracks echoed with the burst of shots and we ducked for cover. The Military Police were summoned as the machine vibrated and gurgled, pierced with bullet holes, spewing a stream of Coke, Orange Crush, and Seven Up. John Machado surrendered without incident. We never saw him again.

It was a strange time. Fort Dix, New Jersey, was in the grip of a persistent cold front and we marched to the rifle range as snowflakes parachuted lazily all around us. We walked through the pines and the snow clung to the trees softly because there was no wind to shake it loose. This enchanting scene contrasted with the stark reality of life as a trainee. One could enjoy the solitude and wonder of nature but at any moment the harassment that is part of training could shatter the reverie. There were many incidents that could serve as an example of this aspect of our experience but one memory is particularly vivid. Once, during a morning formation one of the soldiers whose mother had sent him a dozen doughnuts was forced to eat most of them in front of us. As he stood there coughing up powdered sugar, his cheeks swollen from dough that refused to go down, I wondered; will he be a better soldier for the humiliation and pain? Certainly, Basic Trainees had been warned about the consequences of receiving food from home but some mothers could not help themselves.

My brother Michael was a Second Lieutenant and he was also stationed at Dix and resided in the BOQ (Bachelor Officer Quarters) less than a mile away. He had walked into my barracks once and had torn up my bunk as a joke. I chuckled at the sight. I knew that Michael had to have informed the Drill Sargent of his prank. In his own way, he was informing my superiors that he was nearby. I realized that if I received donuts in the mail I wasn't going to be required to eat them.

Michael picked me up at the barracks after I had eaten my Thanksgiving dinner at the mess hall. He had endured his meal dressed in his blue uniform with other officers displeased with the formalities. "We couldn't even talk for most of the meal," he said. *Tears of a Clown* by Smokey Robinson and the Miracles played quietly on his car radio as we drove away from the barracks. The sky was grey, yet clear, and I stared out the window at the treeless, snow-encrusted asphalt surrounding the dull brick buildings. As always, Mike and I talked about the characters in our neighborhood back home. Nukka Horton whose head was perfectly rectangular and who had one skinny tooth residing in between his two large front ones was the caricature today. "I think he was taken out with vise grips at birth," Michael chuckled.

As we scurried up the stairs and unlocked the door to his apartment in the BOQ, I could hear an old refrigerator clanking in his kitchen. I sat at the table and he made coffee. "The cards are on the counter," he instructed. I began shuffling the deck and inspecting his sparse home. The furniture seemed old, but sturdy. The tiles around the sink were cracked and chipped. I began to wonder as he retrieved the coffee mugs what it was that had always undermined the quality of our relationship, what the tension might be? It seemed that we never spoke about mom. As children, we came to anticipate the grimace that would scar a listener's face when we told them that our mother was paralyzed and required a respirator. To Michael, from that moment on, we fell into a category from which there could be no escape. "You can't get respect out of pity," he'd say. Besides, Mike was all about discretion. One had to gain his trust first before he would open up. He had one very good friend in the army. Roger was the only friend he needed. Roger would be his best man at Mike and Phyllis's wedding and would be the only person he confided in concerning his anxiety as an officer in Vietnam. Our mother conversely placed her condition out to the world, making friends easily and often, boldly exhibiting our misfortune and smiling at the responses. Mike craved privacy, and that was impossible when practically everyone in the neighborhood had a key to your house.

We played Hi-Lo-Jack, drank coffee, and smoked cigarettes into the evening, reminiscing about our time at St. Margaret School. "Saint Maahhgrits," Mike would exaggerate. We laughed to the point of tears when we remembered the ballgame when Pat McGill argued that he was safe at first on a close play. Cruelly, we derived humor from his speech impediment. He had been overruled by most of the players on both teams. In his frustration he screamed, "I eject! There ain't no empire."

Mike locked the door as we departed and I skipped down the stairs to the car. He turned the ignition and stomped the gas before turning on the heat. "I should have ordered you to go warm up the car," he grinned. "You know how tough it is for me to obey orders," I retorted as I rubbed my hands and slid them under my legs. "Besides, I would have forgotten what you told me to do by the time I got down here." "No doubt,' he cracked. "No doubt." As I contemplated our differences on the drive back to the barracks, I understood that it was no surprise that Mike had excelled in the military. On the other hand, I had just graduated from high school and my life had been free and easy all summer. I found the structure of the army constraining. Mike was twenty-one years old and had matured considerably. I was proud of his achievements.

Mike turned down the radio as he gripped the steering wheel with his left hand. "Look, Bernie," he said quietly. "I know you don't like the army and you are against the war. Don't think that I'm thrilled either. I want you to understand that my patriotism cannot be defined by one of your slogans. Sure, I'd like to 'make love not war,' but it's not that simple. I accepted this and now it's my duty to see it through." I did not respond immediately. I opened the door when he stopped in front of the building and thanked him for the time away from Basic Training. "I'm not running to Canada or anything," I replied. "I respect what you're doing."

I scampered up the stairs to the barracks and past the mortally wounded coke machine. Sitting on my bed, I regretted the things I didn't say. Somehow, I felt like I had betrayed my principles by not speaking up minutes before. Mike's integrity made everything he said a validation of firm belief. It was true that I spouted slogans when it came time to express my political point of view. Most troubling was the notion that we responded so differently to our shared tragedy. As I dwelled on my fate, now feeling like the victim of a boring institution, Michael seemed to forge ahead as if he had been liberated. He had escaped the paralysis in our family, if only temporarily.

Chapter Twenty-Seven - 1970

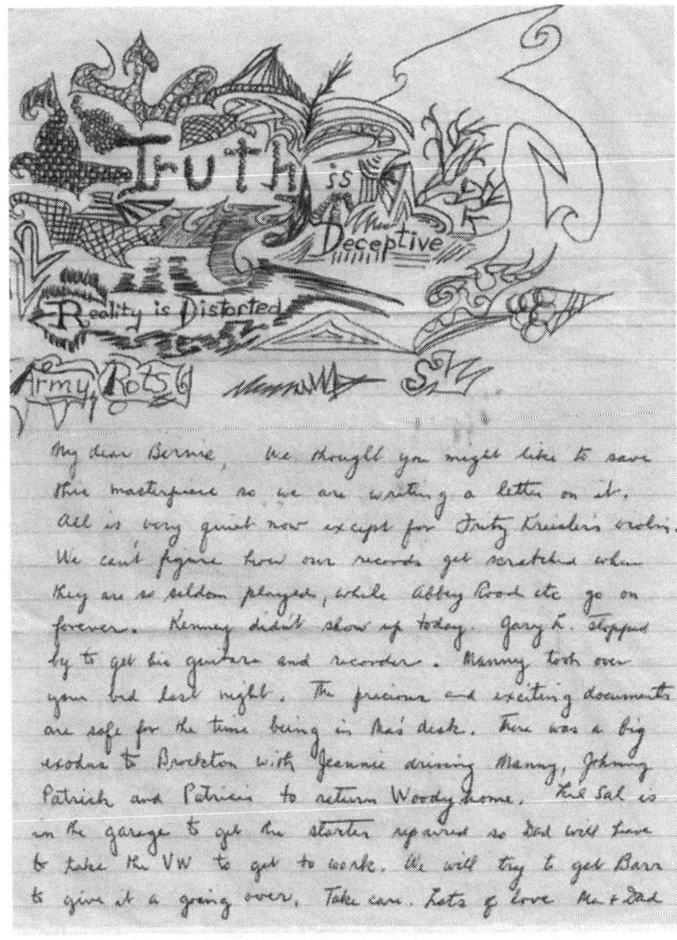

My dear Bernie, We thought you might like to save this masterpiece so we are writing a letter on it. All is very quiet now except for Fritz Kreisler's violin. We can't figure how our records get scratched when they are so seldom played, while Abbey Road etc go on forever. Kenny didn't show up today. Gary L. stopped by to get his guitars and recorder. Manny took over your bed last night. The precious and exciting documents are safe for the time being in Ma's desk. There was a big exodus to Brockton with Jeannie driving Manny, Johnny, Patrick and Patricia to return Woody home. The Sal is in the garage to get the starter repaired so Dad will have to take the VW to get to work. We will try to get Barr to give it a going over. Take care. Lots of love Ma + Dad

Letter from Home to Bernie

When Michael and I entered the army, our cars were quickly expropriated without due process by my mother and father. My 1959 VW became the company car. Luckily, I had very few complaints otherwise. My parents were there for me while I was in basic training and when I went to Fort Sam Houston to be trained as a Medic. They took every call and answered every letter attending to the specific issues I had raised. I inadvertently supplied them with this letterhead while back on leave in the summer of 1970. If I had asked them to come and get me to flee to Canada, they would have arrived in the bus with as many teenagers as could get permission and driven me there, but I didn't want to flee. My father soothed me carefully, never scolding me, but attempting to dissipate my anger and to understand the integrity of meeting my commitments. In his letter, I sensed his gentle humor and his wisdom.

In September of 1970, Michael started a 12-month tour in Vietnam. The discussion between my parents became less contentious. They consoled one another. This dispassionate dialogue concerning his deployment bothered me. I was stationed at Valley Forge Hospital, in Pennsylvania working on the psychiatric ward. Part of my time was spent convincing amputees that life was worth living, and I often used my mother's tenacious pursuit of happiness as an example, with therapeutic results. I worried that Michael would become an amputee or worse. When I telephoned my mom and dad about the political situation in Vietnam, my anger intensified. My tirade was met with a tempered amount of concern. "Bernie," my father admonished, "Michael is a survivor and the best you can do is pray." "And vote!" mom added. Still, every day new amputees fresh off the battlefield would arrive and stoke my fear.

On one of my calls home my mother divulged that Pat's husband was becoming a menace. Joe was only reliable with missing rent and food payments. He was a fixture at the racetrack, standing at the rail urging his horse on, slapping the racing program against his thigh as if he were the jockey. Sometimes, he'd wait for the jockeys to ride their horses in the alley to yell his displeasure. "You were holding back!" he'd yell. Win or lose, he'd end up at the bar afterwards. If he got home at two in the morning and he was hungry, Pat would wake up and cook him eggs and toast. The next morning Pat would be at our house at 7:30 AM, no matter how little sleep she got the night before. My mother and Pat had become very close and Joe's behavior was disturbing everyone.

One night when Joe got way out of hand, Pat retreated to our house with her children. As Joe pounded on the door my father woke up. "Go to bed, Joe, and sleep it off!" my Dad hollered through the door. "I don't want to have to call the police." They ended up calling the police, and my father had to appear at the courthouse to lend credence to the charges. This was one more burden on my dad. He described his feelings on the day of his court appearance:

"**Return to Diary**: *"Now more than ever it is necessary to push to get anything written down. I went to court in East Providence as a witness against Joe Kralik. I wish I could return to my old ability to catch the atmosphere of the place. There are lots of pictures in my mind but the old drunk has less power, less discipline, less desire to be bothered.* ***I don't think I ever wanted to be writing for its own sake."***

When I came home on leave to attend Michael and Phyllis's wedding I cornered Joe. A filter-less Pall Mall cigarette was dangling from his lips. He glanced down at the ground and I could see that he understood why I was confronting him. He was trying to get into his car but I was in the way. "Look, Bernie, I am sorry. It won't happen again. Besides, your brother Michael has already made it clear to me." Without saying a word I walked away.

Chapter Twenty-Eight - An Epiphany

Bernard had been sleeping heavily of late, with vivid dreams. Having left the window shade open the night before, he watched the morning sun slowly rise and brighten until it spotlighted the clothes that hung in his closet. He felt very tired and short of breath, even after his long repose. He got up from bed, slid into his bathrobe, and shuffled up the hall to the bathroom. As he shaved he was aware that he felt different today. There had been a tingling in his fingers these past few days and he had only managed to read a paragraph of *Zane Gray* before falling fast asleep last night. As he walked in to set Marie up, he heard her voice, reverberating as if it was coming from an echo chamber. The grinding of the rocking bed, perhaps, created the illusion. He didn't feel badly, but certainly not normal. "Are you ok, Honey?" he heard her say. "Oh, I am just a little under the weather," he replied.

He did not make it in to work that day. He had an epiphany while driving. He parked his car near the Brown rowing team shack and stared out at the calm Providence River. In his car alone, gazing at the flowering trees on the far bank of the river, the tensions that had festered within him for so long suddenly released in rapid succession. He stopped worrying. The aches and challenges of his body seemed to dissolve, moving away from him. "Relaxation?" he wondered. Had he really been clenching his teeth for 16 years? Why did he hold his breath so often? Perhaps these stopgap measures had been exacerbating his stress all along.

The issues of the moment floated around in his mind, but in a detached, serene way. Mike had come home from Vietnam on emergency leave to attend to Phyllis, who was having difficulties with the final stages of her pregnancy. Pat's car had been hit by a drunk driver and Dad was supposed to call Fred Lawrence, our attorney, on her behalf. My father also had a pulmonary conference he needed to attend on Monday. As he sat, staring out the windshield, he tried to prioritize, he tried to focus, and he tried to care.

It was late morning when he arrived home. He stumbled past my mother and Pat Kralik to his room. Competing thoughts were racing within. He felt compelled to act but before he could another new thought or feeling stymied his attempt. Visions of his workplace reeled. He had parked the car facing in the wrong direction and vomited on the sidewalk. Someone was speaking to him but he could no longer see anyone. The world surrendered to his dreams. He was at work. The lenses of his thick glasses clicked gently as they met the lenses of the microscope. He reached for a slide.

Marie's heart started to churn and she began to hope that he had simply drunk a little more than usual. She could not dismiss the anxiety that rushed over her. She sensed that her world was destabilizing before her, and even her strongest defense, denial, was breached. "Pat, better call Michael," she managed to say. Pat reached Michael at home and explained to him that they thought Dad needed immediate help, even on the assumption that he was just intoxicated. Michael replied to Pat's plea with some irritation. "So, the prodigal son returns," he said, as he hung up the phone.

When he arrived at 56 Ruth Avenue, he found our father sitting on the edge of the bathtub, eyes closed. His hands were mimicking the movement of slides under a microscope. Mike knew instantly that Dad was not intoxicated, but in serious trouble.

Michael helped carry him out to the ambulance that Pat had called, and accompanied him as it sped towards Memorial Hospital, ten minutes away. In many ways, Michael was not unprepared, he had been operating on sheer adrenaline for the past eight months. He was an officer leading a South Vietnamese company of apathetic soldiers through death and destruction before he was notified of Phyllis's emergency. Suddenly he was rushing home because his wife's life was threatened by a difficult childbirth. Flying down Roger Williams Avenue with his father unconscious next to him in the ambulance, he barely had time to recognize any emotion that might have surfaced from the urgency of action.

After he admitted his father, Michael stood in the waiting room trying to cope. How should he feel and how should he respond to this, now? Another tragedy, another emergency, another wound to the heart. He was standing quite still, glaring at the flashing lights of ambulances as they came in bearing those who might live or die, even as his father's fate was already determined. The unyielding obligations of Dad's life were completed, mercifully fulfilled by a massive, fatal coronary. Michael glanced at the blocks depicting the date at the nurses' station. Friday, May 21st, 1971.

Part Three

Days End

Upstairs the children sleep
In dreamless abandon.
We sit together on the steps
Father – mother, husband – wife,

Bound by love's double bond.
The very core of life is here,
Press it quietly to your heart
Lest it slip away from you.

-Marie Mulligan

Chapter Twenty-Nine - The Day After

"The extent to which he had cared for her in every way, even in his darkest times, was massive, and his absence echoed through every part of her day."

Family Gravestone

"I want photos!" she cried, before dissolving back into silence. My mother had stopped eating. She did not make eye contact; she just looked away from me if I tried to start a conversation. Flowers and friends arrived, but her sadness kept most visits short and the bouquets were merely stacked on the kitchen table. Even the cats were subdued.

I was stationed at Fort Ord in Monterey, California, when the Red Cross notified me. I was shocked to hear that Dad had died. I had been enjoying my life in Monterey until then. Surprisingly, more medics were needed in the US than in Vietnam, specifically to deal with the hundreds of thousands of wounded and mentally ill young men and women transitioning back to America. I wasn't going to Vietnam even if I volunteered. In California, I was working nine days on and nine days off, exploring the Los Padres National Forest in Big Sur, and driving a red, green, black, and yellow '59 VW bug.

When I returned home, I could see that the household was operating on automatic pilot, addressing all basic needs quickly and quietly. My father's life insurance, Social Security, and money sent from Meme in England alleviated any financial concerns. My mother's miserable condition led many family members and friends to speculate that her demise would hasten, now that her husband was gone. The extent to which he had cared for her in every way, even in his darkest times, was massive, and his absence echoed through every part of her day.

At the funeral home, we took Mom's requested photos of Dad, framed in flowers with his hands draped over his belt buckle. During the wake, a two-day, eight-hour affair, hundreds of visitors arrived to offer their condolences and kindness. In the reception line, a dark-haired man with hunched shoulders shook Michael's hands and croaked, "So sorry." I looked closely at him as his face came into view. His facial bones were extended and his cheeks stuck grimly around his upper jaw. "Are you Rigor Mortis?" I asked. Embarrassed, he shook his head yes, acutely aware of the nickname that his coworkers had pinned on him.

Clouds of pollen wafted through the air at the cemetery as they lowered his casket into the ground. Sister James Francis stood next to Pat Kralik. I stood with Michael, Patrick, and David. The funeral was well attended. During the reception at our house, after the burial, I showed my mother the pictures. She began sobbing and crying, attracting everyone in the house. "Oh, Bernie!" she stammered. "If I had only known." I knew she was not talking to me, but to Dad. His strong spirit had disguised his frailty until the very end. She stared out the window, despondent and grieving. Periodically she would sob, until she fell asleep into fits of curious dreams.

I taste salt in the wind; the air is sparkling with mist. Flooded with sunlight, the sky is endless and each cloud is cast in shadows of deep blue and yellow. I am walking. The sand is hard under my feet from the exit of the tide. Waves percuss and children squeal and laugh; the sounds foam together and coalesce to form a song. I see you surrounded by sheet music, delicate against your rough wool army blanket. As I approach, you begin to gather your towel and shake the blanket of sand. You are leaving and I am fading, unable to move forward quite fast enough. "Wait for me!" I scream. I am suddenly frozen, my limbs too tired to obey me, and still you move on without and beyond me. I have written a poem for us.

None Will Know

We strolled along the smooth swept sand
Our footprints blended;
The white waves washed where we had walked
Before the day ended.
We made a castle near the rocks,
The tide crept and ebbed away
And all was lost
Many lovers since have played
Beside that sea,
But none will know that we were there
Save you and me.

A heap in my sorrow, I feel cold beneath me, something is catching underneath my dress and my arms are confined. I am contained and unable to free myself; I am in a wheelchair, now, alien and unwanted. The wheels are sinking into the sand as the chair loses balance, flipping me backwards. When once I felt pain, now it is just a reverberation in my skull. The sky stretches out and I feel nothing. Alone, I am being pushed out to sea, by what or whom it is unclear. Waves are crashing against me; I am floating in an iron lung. Water begins to enter the machine; it submerges and the quiet of the water comforts me. I move. I pull my hands out of the machine and pull my body out like a tortoise from its shell. I'm surfacing. Oh, no, no, drat it all. I'm here; awake, in my rocking bed, paralyzed and Bernard, my only love, is dead.

Chapter Thirty - The Decision

"I am going back to that hell-hole and you are coming back here."

Michael and our cousin Tom in Vietnam

My father had been buried for only a week when my friends and I were sitting around his piano. There were about ten of us armed with guitars, spoons, and bongos. I sat on the piano stool next to Manny Fonseca. He had moved into my room when I entered the army; Manny's family was unpleasant, and our home was a refuge for him. My mother did not care particularly what his parents thought. If they wanted to discuss it she would explain why it was appropriate that their child move into our house. Ironically, she never explained it to me and my brothers. Why we should accept our neighbors' children into our house, at our dinner table and into our lives remained unanswered. No one even brought it up. Many teenagers passed through the house after Bernard's passing. Manny was playing the chords while I played the bass line. We sang, "If you ever change your mind about leaving…leaving me behind." Manny would yell out the chord changes at the end of each verse. "C, G, and then F to C," he'd yell before returning to the melody. It was a warm night and the windows were open. As we sang, the trains feeding raw material to Washburn Wire and Okonite Company squealed in the distance. Patrick was playing his stereo upstairs while David and Ray Francis played a board game in his room. When it got late my friends put away the instruments and left quietly, as it was a school night for Patrick and David. Besides, I had to get my mother ready for the night.

After catching her gaze in the kitchen mirror, I entered her room. "I'm bushed, how about you?" I asked cheerfully. She did not answer. Upon turning on the rocking bed I tried again to initiate a conversation, but she seemed lost in thought. My mother was still grieving. "Are you OK?" I asked. She merely nodded her head in affirmation but I knew better. The woman who talked to me about her feelings in excruciating detail was silenced by the magnitude of her loss. I pulled the blanket up to her chin, tucked it under the mattress, and said goodnight. I glanced back at her to see her absorbed in thought. As I sauntered to the bathroom, I could not imagine what she was thinking. Cautiously, I knocked on the door. Something told me to wait a minute, but I pushed through and found it empty. I brushed my teeth, and then walked to my dad's bedroom. Sinking into my father's bed, I inhaled the aroma of pipe tobacco hanging in the air. My father's clothes still hung in the closet and his rack of pipes sat on his bookcase. I quickly drifted off to sleep.

I dreamt that my dad was behind me, with his arms crossed, shaking his head derisively. I was relieved when I was awakened suddenly by her voice. "Bernie!" my mother called, softly through the intercom. I looked at the clock in the moonlight. It was past three in the morning. I stumbled slowly up the hall and into her room. Her eyes were wide open. "Turn on the light, please," she whispered. "What's up, Ma?" I asked wearily. She tilted her head displaying a tired smile. I sat in the easy chair watching her rise and fall. Her voice faltered as she started to speak. "We need to talk," she said. "We have a problem. I want you to get a hardship discharge to take care of me instead of Michael." "Ma!" I blurted. Her suggestion was alarming. She was already beginning to cry as I stated the obvious: "Come on Mom, he will go back to Vietnam in that case. If you choose him instead, then I get to go back to Monterey." It felt as if the rocking of her bed had increased speed. My pulse began to race and my heart was pounding. One always had to be extremely careful while maneuvering around her room. I instinctively rose from the easy chair to touch her mattress as if to calm it down. "He doesn't like me and he doesn't know how to take care of me like you do," she said pleading her case as she wept. I had never refused my mother's wishes. Under the circumstances I wouldn't even consider denying her request. Her tentative hold on the happiness she had worked so hard to achieve was at risk and that potential circumstance withered my resolve. After assuring her that I would start the process of my discharge from the army, I sat back in the chair and watched silently as she cried herself back to sleep. When I was certain that she had drifted off, I returned to Dad's bed. I contemplated this new arrangement while praying fervently that she'd reconsider. Dad's disturbing appearance in my dream had increased my anxiety. What did it mean?

The next day my friends and I congregated once again around the piano in my father's room. My brother met with my mother behind closed doors. Ostensibly, they were going over the funeral bills and Social Security forms but the real point of discussion concerned my mother's decision. Eventually Mike emerged from the room and walked purposefully down the hall. In the middle of our jam session he opened the door and screamed, "Shut UP!" The music stopped and we all sat in stunned silence. He beckoned me with his finger.

I followed him into the living room. He turned to face me. "YOUR mother," he hissed, "has made a decision. I am going back to that hell-hole and you are coming back here. You must be pleased!" I gazed at the floor and replied, "Not really." I quickly raised my head to see his eyes glaring at me. It occurred to me that we were playing the game of polio all over again. However, the stakes were much higher this time. Neither one of us wanted to blink or speak, so we continued to stare. After three or four tortuous minutes, I realized that, as usual, I was no match for him. The anger in his eyes was so disconcerting. I did an about face and walked back to the music.

That night, I pondered the familial roles that Mike and I had developed over the span of our lives. My parents had not named Mike after my father. The convention of naming the first-born after the father had been ignored. Had Fate and Destiny intervened? Is this why I am Bernie? My father's countenance, the memory of his dreadful life and his words; "I can't cure polio; that's a fact!" jarred me. Like Dad I understood that failure was not an option but unlike him it was clear to me that failure was a possibility.

Chapter Thirty-One - Marie's Journey

"She was becoming a destination."

Marie's world had suddenly shrunk because her driver was gone; she could not get out of the house unless an ambulance was beckoned. Her need for company and companionship intensified after the loss of her husband. She was comforted by the fact that she could walk through other people's emotions, exploring their motivations and desires, and safely avoid confronting her own. An excursion through Pat's excitement concerning her children, her husband, or Elvis Presley could take up a whole day. She could navigate the origins of David's "somber tone of voice." Her skill as a conversationalist, gentle debater and confidant became even more acute. She could take a short cut to one's soul by merely engaging in a simple conversation. Eventually, governors, mayors, and political candidates of every political party would pull up to her side with one foot on the wooden railing of her rocking bed, their heads tilted in next to hers smiling broadly into the camera. Initially, politicians stood next to her like they were standing next to a statue or a flag. Inevitably, one by one they would be drawn into her world. Her command of English, French and German facilitated her communication with all visitors. She was becoming a destination. It didn't matter who you were. If one wandered into her sphere of influence, her perpetual curiosity would draw all to her. Patrick, David, and I were obligated to "talk about" our feelings towards one another "now that Dad is gone." Although none of us enjoyed the introspection we all found ourselves surrounding her bed discussing whatever topic she deemed germane to her purpose. "Now, Patrick," she'd start. "We are certainly not asking Bernie to be your father!" One time she whispered for me to come to her side. "Close the doors," she breathed. With the doors closed I stood adjacent to the head of her mattress. "The *curse* arrives tomorrow," she announced with a look of dread in her face. "Ma!" I moaned. "Do we really need to talk about this?" No topic was off limits and no amount of sadness or tears could impede her voyage into the prevailing mood or mindset. She could provoke anger and hostility, but she'd eventually deconstruct those powerful emotions with her tears or laughter. We were all bound in her orbit, oscillating in a fast cycle each day between our feelings and hers.

By the end of July, the bus had been parked in the side yard for 10 weeks. Its promise of adventure had left us. The extra rocking bed remained bolted to the floor and the generator sat on the platform, waiting for a new chapter in its unusual life. No one had considered driving it. One morning in August, I walked in my mother's room to catch her in a rare quiet moment. She was staring out the window at the empty bird-feeder as it balanced on the old elm tree stump. "No birds today, Bernie," she sighed. "We have nine cats now, Ma, and I think the birds are painfully aware of it." "I need to see birds," she said. "I want to get out." I told her that I'd take the bus out for a test drive. "Will you, Bernie? It would mean so much…" she brightened.

Chapter Thirty-Two - Queenie

—Tribune Photos

THE LATE BERNARD J. MULLIGAN stands behind rejuvenated antique school bus he rebuilt to provide transportation for his paralyzed wife.

Dad with Queenie

I pushed open the doors of the 1955 school bus and sat in the driver's seat. I stared through the flat, split windshield into the backyard. The nose of the bus was nuzzled into the foliage of our pear tree and ripened and rotting pears splattered the hood. Someone had named the bus "Queenie". I am sure it wasn't my father; although he always named vehicles after women, he seldom selected something conventional. He would have chosen Matilda or, perhaps, Enid. I turned in the seat to scrutinize the rocking bed, strangely quiet and bolted to the floor. The sun shone through the plexiglass casting its rays on the bed. I imagined passengers seated in the few seats that my father had left bolted to the floor. Curtains that had been hung on the side windows were now flapping in the wind because some of the frames no longer closed entirely. I turned back to the front and opened the glove box to find the registration. It was expired and there was no insurance, nor would there be. My parents did not believe in insurance. Licenses and registrations were already more like guidelines than laws to them. Venturing out with little money and few precautions in a shaky old school bus had been a natural way of life for my father.

I started Queenie up and backed her out onto the street. I rested my hand on the vibrating stick shift protruding from the disintegrating rubber casing surrounding its base. After I drove the bus for two miles or so on Roger Williams Avenue, I parked it back in the same spot under the pear tree. It had not been as difficult as I had anticipated, but the 1955 bus certainly did not handle well. I inspected the tires and found that they were bald and out of balance.

"Well, what do you think?" she inquired as our eyes met in the mirror. "It still runs," I muttered. Eventually, I promised my mother that I would drive one local trip before attending to the tires and the registration. She was gleeful. Then she turned somber; "I miss him so." Over the past few months she had been vacillating between tears of joy and tears of sadness so often that someone had pinned a cleaning cloth for her tear-steamed glasses on the mattress. "I have the money to get new tires," she enthused, "but the title is in your father's name, and we will need to transfer that. I know you abhor the Registry of Motor Vehicles, dear."

The possibility of traveling again invigorated Marie. Her life was changing and she was opening up to new experiences. I had given my mother her first headphone set for her birthday, so that she could listen to music during her muscle rubs and manipulations. John Sebastian had made a record called *The Four of Us* in 1971 and my mother enjoyed listening to it. This was the first music that she listened to on the headphones. "It sounds like the guitar he is finger-picking is right in the room with me," she marveled. The record was a mini folk/rock opera about discovery and travel. The theme appealed to her and I could see in her eyes that she had been thinking about exploration of her own. She asked me if I would be willing to drive to Meadville next summer. "We'll fix Queenie up properly," she assured me.

Mom agreed with me that we should be conservative on our trial trip. After all, it was an unregistered bus, my license was not the proper class, and the tires were wobbling. An assembly of teenagers and young adults gathered in my mother's room on the day of our first voyage. Our first trip without Dad commenced with my mother's transfer from the house to the bus.

Manny and I inserted our arms under her neck and knees and pulled her off the bed and onto the stretcher, while David wheeled the battery and respirator on their coasters. We carried her into the living room with David hunched and pushing the respirator. Denise Daly opened the front door as Manny and I carried the stretcher to the bus. Patrick had joined David, and now the respirator was being carried in short steps right behind the stretcher. When we reached the emergency door we had to raise her, unplug the hose, and pass her off to Ray Francis and Ken Dooley. Patrick and David moved as quickly as possible to the passenger door to ease their load onto the floor above the stairs. Pat Kralik waited to hook her up once she was lifted onto the rocking bed. Once my mother settled in her bed we all took our places. I sat in the driver's seat and looked at the gang of Pat's children, Johnny, Doreen, Joey, and Melissa, and I wondered how this scene might have appeared to them. Kathy Mitchell and Jeanie Ward stood on either side of my mother. Manny sat with me, his back against the dash, and his legs in the stairwell. After my mother's bed was cranked up, squeezing the mattress into an 'S' she looked at everyone and smiled. "Let's go, then!" she proclaimed.

The trip started inauspiciously as we drove on the back streets of East Providence. We even passed an East Providence cop who bleated his siren hello. We were more conspicuous on Route 95, as our highest speed was only 40 miles per hour. The honking and gestures of irritated motorists did not please me like it did my dad. Kathy and Jeanie had to hold my mother onto the bed fearing that the vibration would shake her off. We drove the 30 miles to Silver Spring Pond in a little over an hour. We parked under a thick elm tree that had a rope swing swaying over the water. Coolers and portable tables suddenly appeared and a party atmosphere developed. The teenagers scurried to the rope swing that dangled over the pond, Manny went to the back to quiet the generator, which had not fared well with the vibration, and my mother convened with Pat about feeding the children. From the driver's seat I spotted a policeman entering the park. I felt a twinge of apprehension but was comforted by the fact that he didn't have his lights flashing. To my disappointment, he still stopped next to the bus and pulled himself out of his cruiser, tugging at his belt purposefully.

I pulled the lever to open the bus door. Squinting in puzzlement the officer instinctively asked for my license. He quickly scrutinized my mother as he stood in the stairwell. "How long has this bus been registered to you?" he asked. I fumbled and mumbled until he interrupted me. "You are Bernie Mulligan and I would think you'd remember within a year or so when you registered the vehicle," he growled irritably. "Ma, can you explain everything to this officer?" I pleaded. I knew that lying to a police officer when they held the evidence in their hand was bad policy. I was 14 years old when it was first registered. My mother looked him straight in the eye smiling. "You know this is my first trip out in over three months, officer. It always amazes me how beautiful it is down here." I led the policeman up to her side before walking back to the driver's seat. I could not hear what was being said, but I watched the policeman nodding his head periodically as my mother explained the situation. For good measure, she had a tear rolling down her cheek at a critical juncture of the discussion. The policeman pulled the visor on his hat respectfully and he drifted away from her. Before departing he spoke solemnly; "Well, Mrs. Mulligan, enjoy the rest of your day." He did not even glance in my direction as he swung out the door. Mom stared out her window as the befuddled man calmly drove away in his police cruiser. Smiling at me, she whispered the words, "I'm bloody good aren't I?"

Chapter Thirty-Three - Green Stamps

Reo was a company with significant financial issues and very little brand recognition. In 1955, White Motor Company purchased it, primarily for its production capability rather than its products. Reo stopped making buses soon thereafter. Our ability to get parts for the bus was diminishing, unluckily at a time when it was developing critical mechanical problems. Queenie was 16 years old. So, as I drove the bus home from the tire shop, I ruminated about our options. None were very good. Purchasing six new tires from Devaney Tire on Broadway in East Providence had solved the shaking problem, but the vehicle was leaking multicolored fluids of out of every part of its anatomy. A rainbow of suspicious looking puddles formed in the driveway after parking overnight. I did not want to drive the bus, it had become impossible to manage.

I walked into my mother's room and flopped into the easy chair. "I can't drive the bus, Ma," I admitted. "It has too many problems." I showed her the receipt. She flinched at the price and she noticed the glue-backed S&H Green Stamps protruding out of an envelope. "What are those?" she queried. Ann Regan, who happened to be standing by, piped up, "If you save enough of em' you could buy a blendah or sum-thin." The man at Devaney Tire, who had told me how difficult it was going to be to obtain parts from Reo, was happy to throw some extra green stamps in the envelope as well as a catalogue of available consolation items that could be purchased with them. Marie focused on the currency in the envelope. "Let me see," she said. Ann placed the catalogue on her reading holder. As she turned the pages her excitement grew. The magazine started with items valued at 10-20 books. Each page showcased more expensive and dazzling treasure. Near the end of the stamp catalogue, road worthy Mobile Homes in glossy photos parked next to roadside fireplaces beckoned. The smiling children held up their hot dogs and the blue skies were perfect. Marie began to dream. We had ten books of green stamps, at a cash value of just over two dollars per book. All we needed was 6,000 books! "Does A&P offer green stamps?" my mother asked. "How do we get more of these?"

As I sat in the easy chair, I could feel a sense of hope brightening in the faces of everyone in the room. I somberly interjected a rebuttal to the notion—it seemed too farfetched to accomplish. Yet, as everyone began to suggest ideas, my objections dissipated into the busy chatter of the collective. A plan was formed: buy a Winnebago with Green Stamps. 120,000 green stamps would be required. As each store was called to inquire about their dispensation of stamps, a real campaign began to take shape. Once we calculated the number of books required to replace the old Reo bus, all the teenagers were dispatched to their respective homes. Each one would ply green stamps from their family's coffers. Within a week we had 200 books. It did not take long for the word to spread to the community of Rumford and to St. Margaret's Church. At first, it seemed so implausible that one could buy a $12,000 Winnebago by finding and pasting stamps in a book. Still, my mother's sheer existence challenged plausibility. I wondered how she could remain so vibrant and eager. Neither the death of my father nor the death of Queenie could discourage her.

The many young people in her everyday existence, numbered far greater than her children. These young people fueled her interests and energy with their exuberance and care. "I will NOT be a shut-in," she'd stammer when frustrated. "I despise the word!" she would add angrily. She instructed Patrick to find a cardboard table and set it up in her room. A wet sponge was placed in a bowl and books were stacked in increments of ten in the closet. All production would take place in her room, and tea and cookies powered the effort. By December we had 1,000 books of stamps, and the local newspapers and television started reporting on the story. Many articles appeared in the Meadville Tribune and piles of green stamps arrived daily from my father's hometown. My mother worked the reporters with expertise, displaying her cheeriness and garnering admiration and awe. My father told me once, "You're not allowed to be unhappy until your mother is." Almost everyone who met her felt this to be true.

***

The phone rang. "Mulligan's residence," was my trained answer. One of the things bonding together the twenty people in and out of our house was our standardized telephone greeting. Upon picking up the receiver I was momentarily stunned by a loud, piercing female voice on the line. "What's so important about your mother's paralysis that she should get any money or my green stamps? There are plenty of other basket cases deserving of my money!" the woman squawked. I responded angrily, "Why don't you give me your home address and I'll come over..." Before I could finish my screaming, I heard my mother and everyone around her yelling to me. I held the phone in the air with a hand over the receiver. "Your mutha wants to tawk to whoever it is that you're yellin at," Ann bellowed. As soon as the head-set was placed on my mother the room fell into silence. "You've certainly raised a valid point," my mother cooed into her receiver. There was a pause as my mother listened to the heckler. "It breaks my heart…'" my mother trailed off. "Maybe I should give up my dream of mobility?" she posited to the woman. "I am being selfish aren't I?" There was a longer pause. "I'll have one of the girls give you our address if you insist, but what about the other causes you mentioned?" Another pause ensued. "Bless you, then," Marie said firmly to the heckler, now turned devotee.

It didn't matter if only two or three stamps came in the mail from someone. A letter or card expressing gratitude would be dictated from my mother, and sent out within a few days. Once, I drove four hours to Maine to pick up a book of stamps from an elderly couple. They invited me in for coffee. I showed them photos and newspaper clippings and told them the whole story. They slipped two dollars into my palm as I left. Within a week of leaving the pair weeping, more books of stamps came from Augusta and Portland.

On March 31st, 1972, the *Mulligan Polio Bus Fund* had received enough S&H Green Stamps to fill 2,396 books. Cash contributions of $4,642.00 had been deposited in the East Providence Credit Union, and State Senator Vernon Stromberg, who had been sponsoring the effort, brought in the press. My mother now had days where she rarely took her head-set off. Curious Rhode Islanders were driving slowly by our house, squinting to catch a glimpse of her. The house was crowded with people. Tea, coffee, and Danish were always available, and usually served by one of a swelling number of teenage girls from the neighborhood. Every few minutes or so, one would hear "Mulligan's residence," serving as a salutation and an announcement. Everyone would quiet down. "Ma, it's for you," Kathy Ward hollered. "It's David Howard from the East Providence Post!" Patrick clicked the toggle switch on the wall, and my mother was immediately divulging the latest production numbers.

A&P and Star Market grocery stores both made contributions and although we shopped at A&P, I frequently went to Star Market to make a pick up. One day in April, Ann picked up the phone and announced that it was Joe Dutra. "Who is he?" my mother inquired. Ann promptly replied, "He's a gahd from stah mahkit." My mother looked totally befuddled. "She means guard, you know; g-u-a-r-d, not g-o-d," spelled Ken Dooley. "Take a message." Marie yelled back.

***

We could not wait for spring when we could open the windows. The house was becoming a smoke-hazed surrealistic abode. People were walking through the door at such a rate that introductions were rendered unworkable. So many smokers so few rooms. 'If they could just congregate in the yard,' I thought. Our one bathroom and its flimsy cesspool could not accommodate the crowd. Fueled by black tea and fruitcake, the members of the committee, visiting dignitaries and vendors mingled uneasily through the fog with teenagers, children, animals, toys, and needs. The Jehovah Witness members barged in regularly as my mother loved the debate about *The Day of Reckoning* "Maybe I'd fare better on that day," she'd say.

Ironically, it was only my mother who could escape the crowd and the turmoil. She could legitimately ask anyone to leave the room because she had the option to announce that; "Nature is calling." Everyone would leave in an orderly procession past the mirrors on the doors. Once the doors were closed if one knew how to attend to her needs one could have a quiet conversation with her while the crowd was milling a few feet away. In 1972, I was the only man eligible for entrance into the sanctum. Patrick and David had not been invited in but they could see the day coming when they would be. 'The girls' could enter in twos and threes and all the laughter and gossip would be contained within the walls and doors.

By April it was clear that the goal of $13,000 in green stamps and cash would be met before summer. In May of 1972 the Winnebago Mobile Home was selected and accommodation for the rocking bed had been specified. On May 21st as we sat in the front pew celebrating the Mass on the anniversary of my father's death we whispered about what it would have been like if we had owned a Winnebago while he was alive. We pondered the events of the past year. Mike's safe return from Viet Nam in September, the construction of the deck, and the imminent purchase of the best wheels my mother could have ever imagined. As we sauntered around the parking lot of the church after the Mass we discussed the tax implications and cost of maintenance with Senator Stromberg. "Got you covered," he replied. He knew an accountant that donated his time. He had strong-armed The East Providence Credit Union into contributing $1500 to finance the first voyage to Pennsylvania.

Representative Stromberg also knew the insurance agent, the salesman at Warwick Motors, and the police chief. He always called me "son." He'd greet me in the front yard with a firm handshake and he'd place his other hand on my shoulder looking at me like he wanted to explain something that I could not possibly understand. "Son, I want you know that I don't care if you vote for me. I am doing this because it is the right thing to do" I always sensed that he was in perpetual campaign mode. It suited his personality to be attending events, working the audience and smiling into the camera. One could locate him in a crowd without difficulty—his suits and ties were as colorful as my mother's sheets. He often wore lime green and pure white.

It was arranged that the day of the presentation of the Winnebago would coincide with my mother's birthday. There would be two newspapers present. A photo with Mr. Stromberg smiling, Pat Kralik pointing, and my mother beaming was being choreographed. A bevy of politicians were lobbying for an opportunity to attend the event. Tea bags were being ordered in bulk and Mr. Stromberg knew a caterer that wanted desperately to contribute his staff, his food and his folding chairs. Peter Palagi's ice cream truck would arrive after the presentation. The television crews would set up the night before. Incredibly, the event was being staged as if it were a complete surprise to my mother. "Oh, Wow!" she would exclaim over and over in rehearsal. The newspaper told the story:

To Receive Motor Coach

Realize Marie's Dream; Birthday On Saturday

The dream and hope of a completely paralyzed polio victim, Mrs. Marie Mulligan of East Providence, will come true this Saturday, June 17, appropriately and happily on her 55th birthday.

At a gala public birthday party in front of her residence at 56 Ruth Street, Rumford, at 1:30 p.m., Marie will be presented with the gift she has wanted most — a big, shiny, hospital room on wheels, which will permit her the freedom of occasional travel outside the home to which her affliction would otherwise confine her.

The $12,500 motor coach, fully equipped with a rocking bed and mechanical breathing paraphernalia her infirmity requires, is the gift of countless friends and well-wishers who came to her aid when it was learned than an older, cumbersome bus converted for her use by her late husband was in disrepair and no longer serviceable.

Raised was a total of $13,232.64 to purchase and equip a new mobile unit. Of this, $7,160.64 was in cash donations and the remainder consisted of 3036 books of trading stamps with an equivalent value of $6072, according to Rep. Vernon S. Stromberg of East Providence, chairman of the committee which conducted the fund raising campaign.

There will be a double

(Continued on page 3)

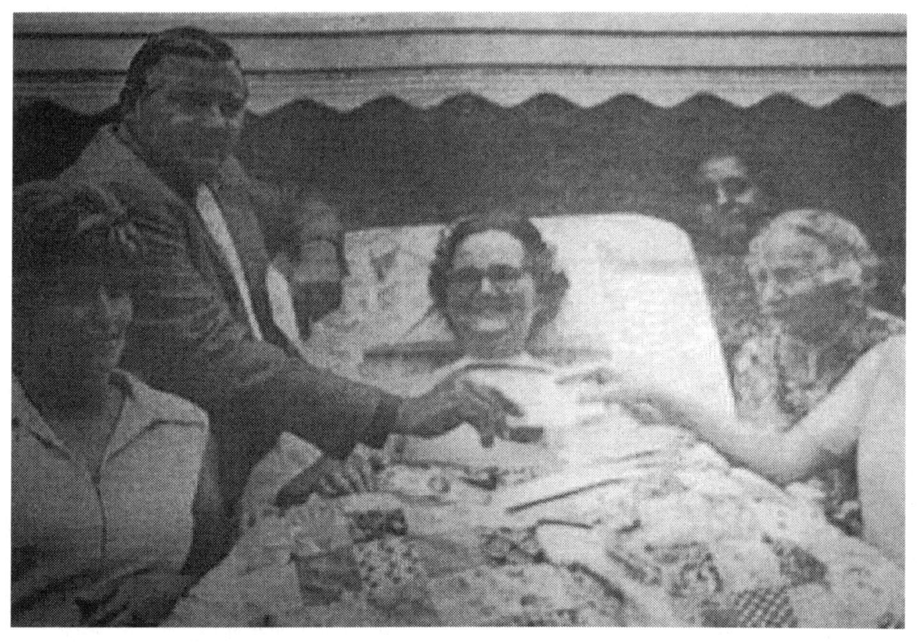

Marie is presented with a check for $1,500 by the East Providence Credit Union. Representative Stromberg is presenting the check

Chapter Thirty-Four - Meme and Marie, En Français

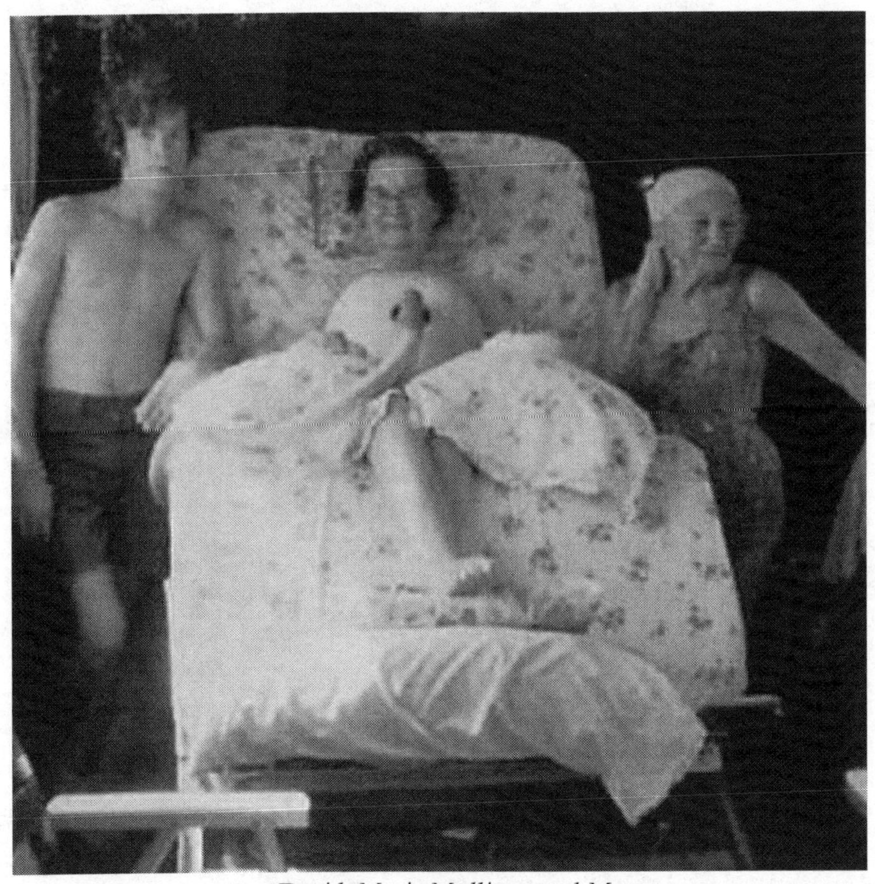

David, Marie Mulligan and Meme

My mother was wheeled out onto the deck as Meme pulled up a lounge chair. I listened to them speaking in French in a serious tone, and although I understood very few words I sensed that they were discussing my father. As Meme picked up her knitting, she suddenly reverted to English. "He is gone, Marie, certainly you need to abandon the obligations of the Catholic Church to be practical." My mother tried to distract her by commenting on the pleasant color that Meme was working into her knitting project. "And those insane end-of-the-world people that you entertain, this God of yours appeals to the basest instincts," Meme continued. My mother looked away. "If I can't believe that I will be with Him again in heaven then I will despair," my mother argued. "I believe in miracles and I believe in God." My mother smiled as she made her point. "Now then," Meme stated sarcastically, "do you believe in that feeble holy man in the Vatican?" My mother addressed the question with an accusatory tone, "Mother, now you are going too far!" That was the end of the conversation.

My grandmother was 83 years old, but so physically limber and passionate about life that we'd often forget and stand idly by as she lifted laundry up from the basement or cut the grass. She spent most of 1972 with her daughter, usually sitting and talking, remarking about the endless appetite of Americans, the stupidity of the Vietnam War, and the cost of medicine. When she cooked, my mother and I rejoiced. Those without healthy tastes had to fend for themselves. My vegetarianism did not offend her in the least. She did not like my bell-bottoms, though. "Are you going to join the circus?" she'd ask me when I walked by with my tie-dyed clothes. She'd play scrabble and card games with mercenary enthusiasm.

She developed a love for the girls who enlivened her daughter's life with their care, gossip-filled chats, and touch. She understood that it was the very classlessness of the neighborhood that allowed for the formation of relationships without preconception. It was remarkable to her that everyone caressed and kissed my mother and called her, "Ma." The unusual nature of the bond that young people formed with my mother was more incredible when contrasted against strangers who would encounter my mother and recoil or avoid contact. In time, Meme embraced the pedestrian nature of the neighborhood. She never stopped pointing out their foibles and lapses in deportment, but their simple altruism and total lack of contrivance or motive inspired her admiration. My mother's belief in embracing life by ignoring the "what if's", compared to most parents, was a wildly popular divergence of opinion on how to approach the world. Plans were hatched. The reckless nature of our household and the willingness of my mother to tap into the precarious naiveté of teenagers imbued excitement into each and every day. Meme, perhaps finally wooed by American enthusiasm, pretended not to know any better.

Chapter Thirty-Five - Bernie Meets Kathy

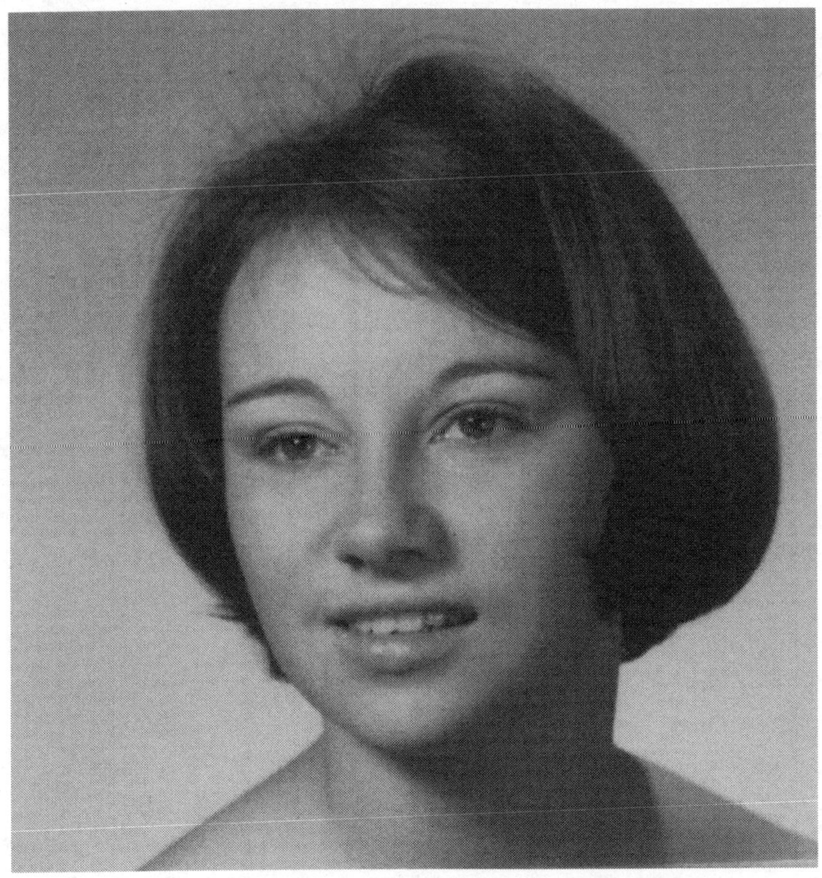

Kathy Rook

When I got out of the army, I was encumbered by a load of new responsibilities at home. I felt isolated even though people surrounded me. It was painful to see them come and go as they pleased while I remained home attending to the needs of my mother and two brothers. When I met Kathy Rook, I informed her that I was obligated to spend a substantial amount of time at home with my mother. Kathy had been a classmate of mine at East Providence Senior High. Her presence and patience buoyed my spirits considerably. We attended the Newport Folk festival together. Over the course of that summer, we fell in love. We talked about music, experimented with cooking and new ideas. Kathy was ambitious and full of opinions, and her home life was difficult. Her father was chagrined by her uncompromising views, and this created friction between them. Over time, she preferred to spend her days and nights with me in my room, listening to the crackling of the intercom as it mingled with the soothing sounds of Donovan, Carole King, and James Taylor. However, Kathy did not integrate easily into the chaos of Ruth Avenue. She seemed aloof and superior to the young adults and teenagers who occupied the house. Her acceptance into the milieu was further deterred by my insistence that she would not physically care for my mother, aside from small tasks, like making tea and writing letters.

One morning as I prepared for work, my mother requested a private discussion. I closed the doors and sat down uneasily in the bedside chair. "What is it, Ma?" I asked cautiously. "What is your long term intention with Kathy Rook?" Before I could answer, she continued, "My mother is coming over and she will be displeased with this arrangement. Representative Stromberg has inquired about it as well, and I think you love her." We agreed, but I could see that my mother was trying to be persuasive. "Perhaps, you should be married. I know you are having sex and she is a good match for you. She is very bright." I had to smile at my mother's use of entrapment. If I said no: I would be denying that Kathy was intelligent, I would be admitting that I was having sex without love, and furthermore, I would be causing Meme and Representative Stromberg moral anguish. "She may have an opinion," I replied sarcastically. My mother countered expertly, "Do you want me to discuss it with her first?" "No!" I replied adamantly.

The day after that discussion, I asked Kathy to go for an evening walk with me in the neighborhood. The sidewalk on Ruth Avenue seemed quiet as we strolled past the Francis' house. We discussed work and I plied her dreams with descriptions of Monterey. "You wake up to the distant barking of seals in the spring, and Asilomar Beach in Pacific Grove has massive dunes, and there is plenty of room there for throwing Frisbee and walking," I rambled enthusiastically. At the corner of Bourne and Ruth Avenue, I knelt down in front of her and pulled out an aluminum beer can tab I had found earlier and proposed. "Are you stoned?" she squealed in astonishment. I assured her that my mind was clear. "It could be a first step towards our life alone," I posed. She did not argue. The night was so still and comfortable. We walked long into the morning, dreaming of California, going on to college, and a peaceful life. "My parents are finally going to have to meet your mom," she yawned, as we returned through the basement bulkhead of 56 Ruth Ave.

We announced our intentions to my mother the next morning. As I feared, my mother authoritatively inserted herself into our marriage immediately. "Bernie, Kathy and I need to converse," she stated. As Kathy closed the door, I reminded my mother to go easy on her. I sat in the living room, strumming my guitar, and watched Pat Kralik's children play outside. When the doors opened, Kathy emerged holding five pages of notes. Though my mother had most likely lead the charge on planning, she was well-matched by Kathy. Our wedding was to be held on the patio outside my mother's room. My mother ordered yellow and pink flowered bed sheets for the occasion. Kathy and Marie reveled in each other's excitement, and their collaboration on the plans went extremely well.

We were married on June 3rd, 1972, the day after a hurricane hit RI. *The Wind* by Circus Maximus blasted from my mother's record player during the ceremony. It was the first outdoor Catholic wedding in the Diocese of Providence, and the Catholic Church, noting my mother's status as a celebrity, delighted in the event. As Kathy and I walked up the stairs, Father Tormey waited as his priestly vestments flapped in the breeze. My mother was wheeled out behind him like a portable altar. The Rook family sat to our left in matching lawn chairs. My friend Steve Barao flitted around taking pictures, and neighbors stood with their elbows on our chain-linked fence, bemused by the proceedings. John O'Neill, my best man, and Denise Daly, the maid of honor, stood beside us as the wind tugged at Kathy's bonnet. My brother Patrick stood behind my mother's bed, recording the event with a super-8 movie camera. Mr. Stromberg smiled broadly in his salmon colored leisure suit, standing next to my mother. He seemed pleased we were conforming to the standards of decency.

After the ceremony, my mother was wheeled into her room and the crowd of onlookers dissipated. There was no procession down the aisle and no traditional music. As I said goodbye to my mother, she whispered, "I will lose you soon." She could not resist inserting herself into the drama. "Ma," I sighed, "It all went according to your plan." Kathy and I joined John O'Neill and Denise Daly on a blissful ride to Point Judith. The next day we took the ferry to Block Island. The hurricane had chased all the tourists away. Kathy and I enjoyed a peaceful, contemplative honeymoon, exploring the island and lavishing in the comfort of Ballard's Hotel.

Chapter Thirty-Six - Another Day, Another Emergency

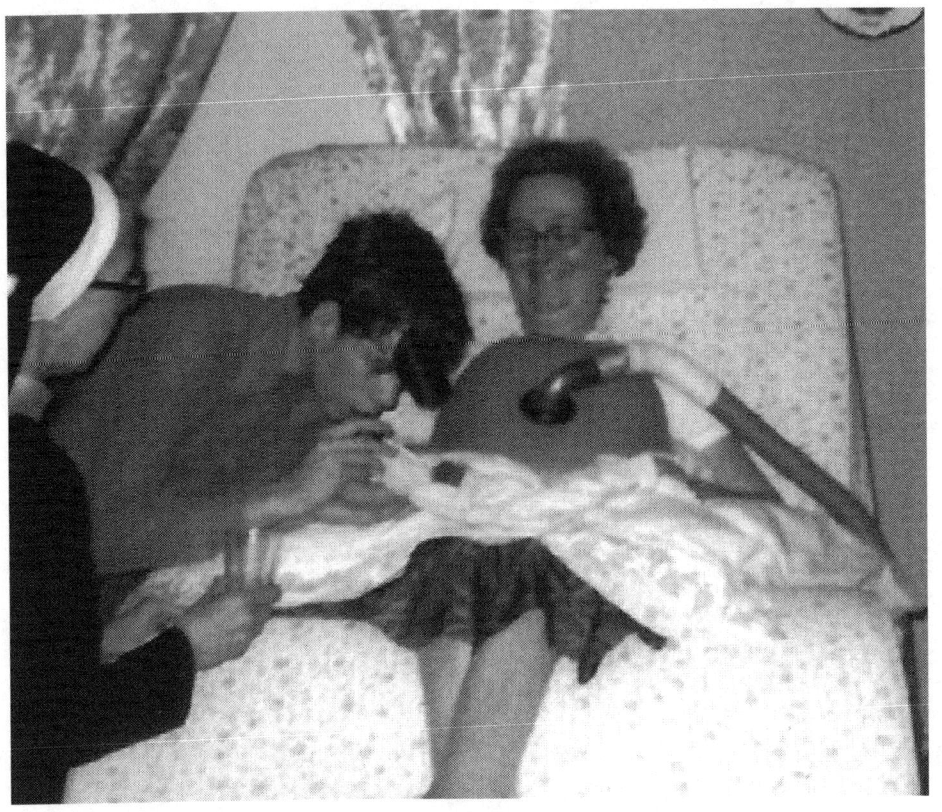

David tending to a newborn kitten, as Sister James Francis assists.

I walked into her room and began to sequester my mother away from the eyes and ears of others. I closed the door that held the mirror that afforded her view to the kitchen. "Do you have new music for me to listen to?" she asked. I had introduced my mother to Procol Harum, the Who, and the The Byrds, so I could always be assured that she would be an avid listener and interpreter. I had purchased and listened intently to the latest Jethro Tull album, and I thought she would enjoy it. She and I stopped everything to spend our time tearing into *Aqua Lung* that particular afternoon. Every note and lyric was dissected and scrutinized. "This is not the voice of an atheist!" she exclaimed. "He is simply rejecting man's insistence that worship conform to the clergy's narrow minded interpretation." As her cohorts were ushered in later, they would be forced to listen to the record over and over. "What do you think?" she'd ask. "Is he an Atheist?" Soon, the house was alive with the question. "He's not the kind you have to wind up on Sunday," Ian Anderson crooned. "What does he mean? What is your relationship to God?" my mother would pose, ravenous for discussion. Ironically, the last thing her teenage audience had just debated was probably taking out the trash or doing the dishes at their home. Something as banal as taking out the trash was the least likely topic Marie would discuss. On any given day, the central question could transition from how to cook macaroni and cheese to one's relationship to the cosmos. Everyone preferred the rumination of eternal life and the existence of God to that of macaroni.

One evening we decided to listen to *Tommy*, the rock opera by The Who. I had just purchased a set of KLH speakers and we placed them facing my mother on stools. I had converted the record to cassette so that we could listen to the performance uninterrupted. My mother had the lyrics on her reading stand and a cup of tea in her holder. The opening horns of the overture blasted and her eyes widened. Listening intently, she immersed herself into the sound, gently assaulting her nervous system. My mother identified with the storyline of the protagonist's isolation. His blunted senses were at first a burden, then a challenge, and eventually a deep resource of strength and power; the tale seemed to resemble her own transformation from the iron lung to the freedom of travel and the intimacy of human comfort. The English setting and accent of the artist only enhanced the experience through familiarity. As she journeyed through the characters; the Doctor, the Acid Queen, and Uncle Ernie, the smile on her face solidified, her head moved to the beat, and she closed her eyes. The strident and angry chords of "I'm Free" filled her room confirming the notion that freedom was possible, despite the most inhibiting of circumstances. The final song, "Listening to You", with its metaphor of music as the language of the gods, made her laugh. She was delighted that Pete Townsend had left the message so ambiguous that she could speculate unfettered about its meaning during the discussion after the performance. "Play "I'm Free" again!" she demanded smiling. "That song is so powerful."

My mother began to write prolifically in 1972, interviewing relatives, inquiring about and finding documents. Her ambition was to write her story and express the creativity that motivated her to continue appreciating life. Ironically, the one subject that separated her from everyone else on the planet eluded her scrutiny. Her struggle with the onset of polio and its aftermath would certainly be the most dramatic part of her story. Yet, she would discuss the iron lung and her three years of isolation reluctantly. "Ma, that's the story. Getting a Winnebago, your life in Chapin, that's what's important," I'd advise when she asked me to edit. Nonetheless, she stuck doggedly to the mundane description of ancient family members, cataloging their jobs, their names, and their affiliations. She dictated about England's kings, queens, and dukes. She researched the Mulligan family history like a scholar. The teenagers would write feverishly at the desk at the bottom of her bed. She had no intention of chronicling the wretched life she experienced in the hospital. By digging and pushing, I would glean her story, but I always knew that she did not want anyone else to think about it. My mother did not enjoy the pained expression of listeners as she described her ordeal. Having developed an acute aversion to pity, she tried to avoid the inevitable gasps and sighs that would escape from her audience if she told the polio story. Nor was she comfortable with the constant mention of her virtue of courage. My mother had taught me that there is "no such thing" as an inappropriate inquiry and that knowing another human required an understanding of their feelings and motivations. Thus, her fear of discussing polio, the grimace on her face when she was forced to recollect did not deter me. She confided in me inadvertently as I rubbed her back or as I filled her scotch glass. However, even as her words detailed the horror, I never quite assimilated the essence of her torture. I persevered in the quest to understand, but largely to no avail. I could not even imagine a life of paralysis, with its cruel limitations—a life that rendered her one mechanical failure away from expiration.

The cessation of the Green Stamp Drive had left a considerable void of stimulation. My mother filled the time with her research and writing. The effort to write mingled with the planning of meals and household chores, and attending to the ever-increasing animal population. The ranks of teenagers and young adults had grown substantially. Most of them had become scribes. "How do you spell 'fortuitous', Ma," a scribe would ask, pens stymied mid-sentence while tea was being poured and music filled the air. My mother battled the prospect of boredom's suffocation by orchestrating the chaos she had lured into our lives. Our recently adopted St. Bernard drooled incessantly on the newly acquired wall-to-wall carpeting. Pat would be cooking as her children played. My brother David made tea and served it to his friends. Patrick played the piano in his room, recording a soundtrack that would accompany the movie he just completed, using Ken and Barbie dolls. Kathy and I lived in the basement, coming and going through the basement bulkhead. Cats roamed inside and out, bringing in dead birds and rodents. Ray the Mailman sauntered in for an hour or so each day while Meme worked over crossword puzzles under the willow tree. An army friend of mine, David Comartin, visited for three months with his beautiful girlfriend, Leslie Ferm, occupying the basement with Kathy and me. They found the pace of life at Ruth Avenue exhilarating. They became enthusiastic participants, scribing, feeding the cats, and answering the telephone, "Mulligan's residence."

One morning at this time, my mother received a call from Grandma Mulligan in Meadville. They had been speaking on the phone frequently, regarding the story. Marie's bed was rocking up and down as Pat and I waited to set her up. These calls could go on for quite some time. A scribe had already arrived eager to take notes. David Commartin and Leslie sat with Kathy at the kitchen table, all in queue for the bathroom which was occupied by my brother David. "Mother, it is so nice to hear your voice," she gushed into the receiver. Suddenly, the headset jerked out of position on her head, knocking her glasses off. As the rocking bed shot up the head set vanished. The telephone cable had been grabbed by the fan-belt and was coiling around the rocker arm. The headset became firmly inserted into the steel frame of the bed. The bed itself began to move backwards, slamming into the windowsill behind her. Frantically, David and I grabbed at the cable, unwinding it as quickly as possible, while trying to slow the advance of the bed out the window. Leslie handed us a knife so we could cut the cable but the cable was taut and moving. Everyone was screaming and my mother was pleading. It was as if the rocking bed were alive as it began to pound viciously into the windowsill and wall, scarring the wood and inciting fear. Patrick came down the stairs from his room. "Help us, Patrick," I yelled. He surveyed the situation seeming almost detached. Patrick reached for the switch on the side of the bed, stopping its destructive force. Within ten seconds, he had unwound the cable, returned the rocking bed to its rightful spot, and then turned the rocking bed back on. It was as if the air had been drawn out of the room. We all froze like statues in our battle stations in stunned silence. We were all so grateful for Patrick's incisive thought and action. "Pat, I think we better look into some new wallpaper," my mother announced as Patrick returned to his bedroom. "What about Grandma?" I asked. "Don't you think we should call her back?"

Chapter Thirty-Seven - Patrick

I eased the screen door open. Once inside the house, I squeezed out of my shoes and placed each shoe quietly on the welcome mat. The floor was creaking audibly under the weight of the rocking bed as I felt my way around the darkened kitchen. My mother's voice breached the quiet when I reached the doorway to her room. "Where is he?" she sniffed. "I couldn't get him out," I whispered. Stepping up to her bed I instinctively found her hand and covered it with mine. "Oh Patrick," she wailed. I shuddered at the dramatic outburst. "Come on, Ma," I pleaded. "This will pass and he'll be home tomorrow." "Set me up. We need to talk," she commanded in a steadier voice. I shut the bed off, placed her chest-piece on, and plugged the hose in. As I cranked her bed into a sitting position our eyes met. "Well, what happened?"

"I drove up to the Foxboro State Police Barracks last night after you received the call from Patrick. The state trooper at the front desk was nice. He actually apologized for the inconvenience. 'If it was up to me,' he said. 'I'd let him go home with you. It's a serious matter, though, Mr. Mulligan.' He showed me into the back where Patrick sat crying in a cell that reminded me of an old cowboy jail. 'Get me out of here!' Patrick repeated several times as I approached him. I told him I would try. I met the arresting officer and he showed me a joint and two pills in a plastic box. "Where are his parents,' he asked. I told him that our father was dead and that you were paralyzed from polio. 'How old are you?' he continued. I told him I was twenty years old. He rolled his eyes. 'I can't release him to you.' He brought the box with us as we walked into a bland, windowless room. He collapsed into the chair behind a grey metal desk and asked me if I knew what kind of pills they had found in Patrick's pocket. 'Looks like Benzedrine,' I said. 'We used to get them prescribed to us when I was in the army.'

My mother gasped. "He IS in trouble."

"Well, Ma, not necessarily," I replied. "It turns out that the trooper was stationed at Fort Sam, in Houston, Texas, as an MP at the same time as me when I was in medic training. We commiserated a bit. Then he took the amphetamines out of the box, dropped them on the floor, and crushed them into powder under his boot. Patrick is being charged with possession of a gram of pot and tailgating a police cruiser at eighty miles an hour. He will be arraigned tomorrow. We need to get our lawyer up there."

I made tea and sat in the easy chair. She asked me to put some music on. "We never did talk about giving Patrick to the Cauleys'" she said. "It just happened. He is so different from the rest of you. He needs me so much. I could never abandon him again."

***

Patrick's behavior as he grew into his late teens exhibited a lack of boundaries and the absence of a healthy sense of self. After most of his indiscretions, my mother would make remorseful comments about his childhood separation. With the explosion of events and unforeseen circumstances occurring after the onset of polio, it is likely that Patrick's transfer out of the family was instinctive. Gladys Cauley had babysat each of us at various times, and she was an obvious person to ask the favor of. There were no legal actions taken to place Patrick in the custody of another family. There was no logic for Patrick's reassignment as the third born, either in our family history or for religious reasons. No explanation was made. My father often mentioned Patrick's infirmities in his diaries. Support for our mother was already in a frantic shortage. Perhaps, that was the rationalization: he was not a healthy baby, and he needed extra care. Michael and I didn't need much assistance and David, as a baby, needed more than someone outside of the family could be asked to provide.

Patrick and David were strikingly different. In their bathtub photo, David seems to be splashing in the throes of emotion, while Patrick stares in bemused calculation directly at the photographer. Blond and thin, he differed from all of us physically. Patrick's physical features came from the Cooper side of our family. His slim build and long face were traits of theirs. He was so limber that he could fold his feet behind his head and walk on his hands while we watched in awe. Patrick had no perceptible qualities that were like ours.

At seventeen, the mutual interest between Patrick and the teenage girls who came to our home became disruptive. He was attractive, charismatic, neat, and particular. In his room, his stereo, easel for painting, and black-light cryptic posters intrigued them. My mother watched uneasily as the girls that she cared so much for became enamored of him.

While our father was alive, Patrick was a constant source of controversy. Patrick was only fourteen when he stole Dad's car and was retrieved from the Seekonk Police Station by my friends, Ken and Susan Dooley. Our parents were in Meadville at the time. Once he made a plaster mold of his genitals, only to find the process of extricating the mold so painful that we had to take him to the emergency room. Ma and Dad felt so guilty about their abandonment of Patrick that they had difficulty disciplining him. "Poor Patrick," Mom would sob when the police brought him into the house. "We deserted him and now we see the result." When I told our mother that Patrick's room had blinking orange lights, courtesy of the Rhode Island Department of Transportation, she simply asked me to return them when it got dark.

At the height of the green stamp drive, Patrick was arrested for tailgating a Massachusetts State Policeman at eighty miles per hour. Our lawyer, Fred Lawrence, had to work pure magic to get the charges dropped. It certainly did not hurt to have my mother make a plea that she needed Patrick to help at home, and that his behavior was a result of his difficult childhood. Contrary to my mother's testimony, he was not particularly helpful. He was self-absorbed and unconscious of his effect on others. I had been working at the psychiatric ward and I recognized some sociopathic tendencies in him. He never adhered to admonishment. Chastising Patrick was a complete waste of time. We didn't know about attachment disorder at the time, but even if we had known, it would have been little consolation.

***

As the Winnebago disappeared down Ruth Avenue for its cross-country voyage, I looked at my wife, Kathy, and smiled. Even though we had to share the house with Patrick, twelve cats, and Brandy the

St. Bernard, the prospect of spending time at home unfettered by my usual responsibility to my mother was exciting. We decided that we had to set some ground rules for Patrick.

That evening, Patrick sat down with me at the kitchen table. We started to discuss curfews and responsibilities when he was joined by his girlfriend, Kathy Mitchell. He quickly changed the subject. "I'd like to have a party," Patrick announced quietly. He wanted to have the party on a night when my wife and I would not be home. I glanced at Kathy Mitchell. "Are you going to be there?" I asked her. My mother and I were very fond of her, and when she said that she would be, and she agreed with Patrick's statement that the intention was to have a small get together with their friends, I accepted their plan.

My wife, Kathy, and I decided to spend that entire day pretending like we lived alone. Her parents were out of town, and we were to stay in their home that night. We packed lunches and drove to Horseneck Beach where we plopped a blanket on the sand in the dunes. I was reading and Kathy was knitting. As the summer crowd began to dissipate, we packed up the car and took the back roads to Seekonk. We ate dinner at Lum's Restaurant before retreating to the quiet of her parents' house in Riverside, about fifteen minutes from my mother's house. Afforded rare hours of solitude, Kathy and I reflected upon our plans of moving to Monterey, California, and attending college. In our minds, we were already thousands of miles away from Ruth Avenue.

***

Two policemen crashed through the side door, yelling, "Where's Delatore?" Kathy Mitchell found herself frozen at the bottom of the stairs. Her friends Monica and Joey gaped at her as the partygoers scattered around them. "I know where to hide," Kathy whispered. They scurried up the stairs and found the small doorway to the eaves. Crawling in one by one, closing the door, and slumping against the storage boxes, they held their breath for a moment and listened. The sound of the cops slamming and breaking furniture, dishes, and doors transitioned to complete silence. The cats bounded into the bushes outside. Below the eaves, in the kitchen, the two policemen were talking. The three above put their hands over their mouths, shutting their eyes and listening. "Look at this," one of the officers laughed, "little Miss will have to come to the station, after all." Kathy's heart paused. They had found her purse on the kitchen table.

***

In the kitchen at her parent's home, she groaned as she handed me the phone, "There's a problem at your mother's house." It was Kathy Mitchell's stepfather and I could hear him yelling as she handed me the receiver. "I can't find my daughter," he fumed. "I can tell you that there were several East Providence cop cars at your house," he continued. When he told me that a shot had been fired, I felt my heart sink. "Was anyone hurt?" I asked. "How the hell should I know?" he screamed into the receiver. "They won't let me in!" I assured him that I would be there in a few minutes to sort things out. As Kathy and I drove to the scene of the party, I could feel my temples pounding. I pulled up to the house and was met by Gary Diaz, a high school classmate of mine, who had recently become a policeman. He smirked knowingly as he shook my hand. "Your brother Patrick is down at the station with several others. There were about fifty kids playing loud music and drinking beer. We responded when a neighbor complained. A beer can was thrown at one of the officers and that's when things got really bad," he reported calmly. "I heard that a shot was fired," I said as evenly as I could. "No one was hurt, right?" He told me that Ronnie, a hotheaded officer, had fired a shot in the air to stop the partygoers fleeing through the backyard. "Some small party!" Kathy hissed. "You can't just let this incident slide," she warned. I did not respond to her because I had not thought that far ahead. "We are interested in one character in particular," Gary said. "His name is Delatore. You can't miss him. He has a tattoo that says 'fuck cops' on his right arm." "Some friends your brother has," Kathy commented. "Gary, how many are down at the station?" I asked.

"Five or six, including your brother and his girlfriend," he replied. I asked Kathy to assess the damage and clean up what she could while I went to the station.

As I drove, my nose started to bleed and my head throbbed. The East Providence Police Station was a short two miles away. I pulled into the parking lot and I gathered myself together before getting out of the car. I thought of my dad and how he had to deal with unforeseen circumstances. "Your life is not your own," he'd complain. "But if Patrick's behavior is unreasonable, why should it affect me?" I wondered. The need to be locked in the present, the need to be rational, the need to subvert the anger I was feeling prevailed. I was committed to solving the issue in front of me. The absurdly unnecessary cause of it had little bearing on dealing with the situation. It was eleven o'clock at night, and my teenage brother and his girlfriend were in jail. If I could secure their freedom, then that was what I had to do. When I finally thought I was ready, I got out and slammed the door so hard that the side mirror cracked. I ran up the stairs mumbling to myself, "Don't be angry". Entering the station, I walked up to the counter and recognized Mr. Andrade, who I used to deliver newspapers to, and who lived on our street. He was the chief of police. He took me aside and shook my hand. "Son, your mother would be very upset if she knew what transpired at 56 Ruth Avenue this evening." He sat me down and continued. "There are two things that you need to consider," he whispered firmly. "One, your brother is being charged with disturbing the peace and we are releasing everyone except Delatore who will be charged with assaulting a police officer. The other thing that you need to understand is that you need to control that house. There were drugs and beer and I will not allow that to continue. Do you understand me?" His voice had escalated and he was staring at me. "Yes sir," I replied. "Your nose is bleeding, son," he smiled as he commented. "I know." I moaned. "It feels like my head is going to explode."

Patrick and Kathy Mitchell were brought out shortly. Neither would make eye contact with me. They could see the pulsation of my temples, as the strain of being reasonable and controlled manifested itself in the clenching of my jaw. They remained silent until we got in the car. "I suppose you're going to take the cops' side," Patrick sulked. "Are you OK, Kathy? Your stepfather is really pissed," I said with calm intensity, ignoring Patrick's lame attempt to access my anti-establishment sensibility. Not a word was uttered on the five minute drive home. When I parked the car in front of our house, the side mirror split in two and fell to the ground. My headache was gone but my anger was beginning to well up. Harry, Kathy's stepfather met me at the gate. He looked at Kathy and instructed her to go home. I told Patrick to go in the house and help with the clean-up. "What kind of shit are you trying to pull here?" he screamed at me. His face was inches from mine. Suddenly, I snapped. He was pointing his index finger in my face. I grabbed it and bent it back until he was on his knees in front of me yelling in pain. "Your daughter did nothing wrong, but you should probably talk to her brother Jackie, because he was yelling at the cops too. My mother and I think your daughter is great. We are not happy that she is seeing Patrick." I bent his finger further. "I am not a child, and I won't be spoken to like that." As I let go of his finger, he could see that yelling at me was the wrong choice, so he quickly apologized. Eventually, we shook hands. Before leaving Harry looked at me and told me that my nose was bleeding.

Kathy and I sat at the kitchen table quietly. Patrick had fallen asleep in his bed. I looked in the mirror at my mother's empty rocking bed. I knew she would not be angry when we told her, but sad. Beer cans and cigarette butts had been collected in several paper bags by the door. One side of the sink was filled with broken dishes and the other with cold, soapy water. Kathy was crying. There was a knock on the side door. "What now," I thought. I opened the door and I was confronted by a husky young man. He had a yellow sleeveless t-shirt on. I turned the outdoor light on and stepped outside closing the door behind me. He looked at me and I could see that his eyes were bloodshot. He had a contusion on his cheek. There was a tattoo visible on his right deltoid but I could not read it. I thought to myself: "This must be Delatore." "I want to talk to Patrick," he mumbled. I could see that he had a fat lip. "We gotta get our story straight." I asked him if he was who I thought he was, and he confirmed my suspicion. Sounding as authoritative as possible, I stated, "Patrick has already given his statement to the police and it would be stupid for him to contradict it." The stocky Delatore tried to push past me. My heart stopped. This was no middle aged scrawny man like Mitch's stepdad, and I did not have the means to confront him physically. "Look, man," I said with as much conviction as I could muster, "Patrick is asleep and you look like you don't want to go to the station again." I stood between him and the door. With his fists clenched at his sides he turned away. "You tell Patrick that it was Jackie Mitchell who threw the beer can and not me and he knows it!" He turned and limped away muttering. The cops had worked him over pretty well. I reached for the door with shaking hands and dropped in the chair across from Kathy. "Who was that?" she asked. "No one, really," I replied. Kathy got up from her seat and brought me a washcloth with ice. I put the ice on my nose. "What are we going to tell your mother?" Kathy asked. "The truth," I said as I tipped my head back. "The truth."

***

Weeks later when my mother and the group had returned, I was still in the midst of an uneasy tension regarding the events of the party. Sitting on the stairs while looking down into the living room, I heard the melancholy sound of Patrick's piano above me. I slouched against the wall and closed my eyes. The sound of a melody trickled into my awareness, and expanded with added waves of accompanying minor chords. The two steps leading to my bedroom had always been safe refuge in their loftiness, a quiet perch to observe the storms that passed below. For thirty minutes, I let the music soothe me. I had almost fallen asleep when his playing intensified. The minor chords were overcome by major sevenths and the melody disintegrated. Over the last two days a chorus of family members, friends, and lawyer had urged me: "Talk to him." I was wrestling with that advice. Everyone wanted the tension to subside, and looked to me to solve it—but I was already shouldering all the needs of my mother. I could not fix everything; I certainly did not know how to fix Patrick. His condition seemed to be at a critical point—a moment when he needed to be reached by someone; this was all the more difficult because he respected almost no one. His conviviality at times could imply deference, but it usually revealed a way of greasing the family's gears to get what he wanted. I had conjectures about who he was, and why, but our relationship wasn't remotely like a parent and child. How could I explain to him where he was going astray? I wasn't perfect, and I too struggled with my emotions and frustrations. Any attempt I made would be ignored. I was a familiar character, and a rescuer at times, but not an authority figure. We listened to music together. We discussed films, books, and bands. I envied his freedom, and I resented him for the responsibility of mine he had become.

Here on the stairs, I just wanted to listen. The music informed me. Repeating a progression on the bass notes, he piled each movement onto one another by holding his pedal down. I opened my eyes and looked at the stairs as if I might see the music laid out in front of me on each step as a code, each note representing a word to get through to him. Suddenly, the music stopped. I waited for the melody and softness to return; instead the sound of Patrick banging the keys with his fist filled the stairwell. When he stopped pounding, he slammed the piano shut and screamed, "Pigs!"

I retreated from my roost quietly, down the stairs and into my mother's room. She was fast asleep. The gentle rise and fall of her chest-piece, the quiet crackling of the intercom, and the gurgling of her new fish tank calmed me. She had been through so much these last few days. "As difficult as these times are," I thought, "they do seem to add some energy to her. Emotional mobility, maybe." She had told me once that some of her dreams were entirely in French. As I gazed at her I wondered if she was dreaming in French, and if her dreams ever calmed her anxiety. "Are you walking?" I whispered.

Chapter Thirty-Eight - Maiden Voyage

"Now, as she sped down the road, she was surrounded by conversation and action."

Marie in the Winnebago

On June 18th, 1972, at 5:30 AM, the Winnebago, affectionately named "Pooh", was fully packed and ready to leave. A bold trip to California had been planned, with many stops along the way. Marie Mulligan, Meme, Pat Kralik, Joe Kralik, Joey Kralik, Johnny Guy, my brother David, and Ray Francis were on board. Pooh, equipped with power steering, air conditioning, and an eight-track player, promised a comfortable and trouble-free ride. Yet, after a sumptuous breakfast in Nutmeg, Connecticut, the wipers and defrosters ceased operation and stirred up a familiar feeling of apprehension. Joe Kralik, the crew's driver, made several attempts at connecting a new fuse before the wipers began to sway again. He then drove the Winnebago expertly onto the highway, and when they pulled off the New Jersey Turnpike at Cherry Hill for lunch, my Mother began to appreciate Joe's talent. It had been raining all day, but even without wipers and defrosters when the fuse first blew, Joe had managed very well. However, she worried about how his drinking and mischievousness would affect the trip overall. "Why can't he just settle down?" my mother wondered. Upon braking suddenly at one point, Meme's small body sailed into the side of Marie's bed. She picked herself up off the floor and asked for the Yellow Pages. "Meme, what do you need?" Marie asked. "I will need a good lawyer!" Meme retorted, amidst laughter. Outside her window, as Pat fed her lunch, Marie watched a red cardinal flit around a young pine tree. The red bird contrasted sharply against the dark needles. The bird reminded her of a daddy-long-leg spider that she would see occasionally when she was in the iron lung. She would ponder that spider's existence for hours as it feasted on the flies that buzzed around the ward. As the cardinal flew away, she watched the branch oscillate, free of the bird's talons, and she noted that no matter how busy her life had become she still existed firmly in the moment. The years of hospital confinement had trained her to observe and record every second of time, carving drama out of the monotony of convalescence. Now, as she sailed down the road, she was surrounded by conversation and action. As her fellow travelers settled into their places, gazing out their windows, she scrutinized their most minute movements: David drumming his fingers, Ray resting his chin in the palm of his hand, Meme smiling while she knitted, Joe staring out the windshield as the wipers clicked like a metronome, and Pat with Joey on her lap, humming to the sound of the music playing on the eight track player.

The Winnebago's first stop was in Odenton, Maryland, to visit a woman who had been a reliable friend to Marie during her time as a new mother at the army housing complex. Pooh pulled into Mrs. Moll's house at 5:15 PM. Marie could see the shock and sadness on her friend's face as their eyes met. The hesitancy of Mrs. Moll, grappling with greeting protocol, was so familiar to Marie that she responded reflexively with a joke. "My God you've aged," Marie exclaimed. They both chuckled and smiled. Mrs. Moll's two sons, Bob and John, brought lawn chairs and their two bulldogs into the bus. Joe joined them both in enthusiastic drinking and banter. John became increasingly intoxicated and obnoxious. His moronic, slurred speech drowned out all meaningful conversation. Meme cast looks of disapproval towards her daughter—John was another ignorant American for Meme to despise. Marie tolerated him uneasily. Each weary occupant, including Mrs. Moll and Bob, eventually urged John out of the Winnebago. After a few hours, he relented and stumbled out the door. Everyone found a place to sleep, still stunned by the unexpected ugliness that had marred my mother's visit with her friend. As if to accentuate the uncomfortable experience, John, still drunk, pounded on the door at 7 AM. Meme could not contain her contempt any longer. "You are a right bastard, aren't you," she snarled. John responded by stumbling back to the house in drunken indifference. Pat hastened the crew to make a quick departure. Mrs. Moll came out to apologize, and my mother assured her that seeing her was worth the trip. No one else aboard agreed with that assessment.

After visiting Washington, D.C., and stopping in Falls Church to fix an auxiliary tank, Joe steered the Winnebago towards the Blue Ridge Parkway. When they broke through the low hanging clouds into the sunshine, little Joey remarked, "I can't believe I'm in heaven!" My mother shared the sentiment, her face beaming at each mountain they passed. Pooh traversed the Missouri, Ohio, and Mississippi rivers. The travelers interacted with curious campers at a camp called "Covered Wagon". She marveled at the garish, glowing signs of endless burger joints and late-night diners between each destination.

The Winnebago was parked in the shade of the huge oak trees in Oakley, Kansas. After dinner, everyone sat around her bed as Meme told a joke. "He opened the door," Meme exclaimed, "and told the policeman to 'Piss Off!'" Even though the joke was not particularly funny, the British expression, 'Piss Off', triggered an explosion of mimicry and laughter from Meme and Marie. As my mother laughed, she started to feel a strain. Her breathing had become difficult even when she was rocking. The Thompson Respirator system and her rocking bed were the only two means of breathing. That night, as she fell asleep, she hoped that the problem would remedy itself.

She opened her eyes in the dull light of dawn as her floral sheets whorled in a blur before coming into focus. She felt strained and anxious; the air was thin and weak. She began to worry. "Someone should be near me, checking the function of the rocking bed," she thought. The inside of the Winnebago seemed dreamlike. Could it be that she was not fully awake or was it that the lack of oxygen had loosened her grip on reality? She had felt this way before, countless times, but the urgency of the challenge to breathe consumed her with such fright that it might as well have been a new concern each day. "Pat!" she croaked. "I can't breathe." Pat and David had to shut off the rocking bed, fasten her chest-piece and plug her into the Thompson Machine before she became comfortable enough to sleep. Now whenever she laughed, she felt anxiety creep into the joy.

Circumstances dictated that a visit to Thompson Respirator Company in Boulder, Colorado would be beneficial prior to continuing on their way to California. The factory representative had been contacted and they were prepared for the visit. As my mother viewed the landscape of the Colorado prairie and as her breathing became more comfortable, she wondered about the house, the cats, the dog, and Patrick. She thought how quiet and peaceful Ruth Avenue must seem with most of the occupants away. She imagined the playing of guitars, the routine of Bernie and Kathy's commuting, the cooking of vegetarian meals, and the sipping of wine. She could see the Rocky Mountains on the horizon as her hearing dulled. Marie had never experienced elevation like this. Her homesickness dissipated as a grey and orange cloud that covered Denver came into view. "Is that smog?" she wondered.

Soon they were past Denver and back into the untamed mountain wilderness. Marie had been rendered nearly deaf from the altitude. For two days everyone had to yell to communicate with her. The road to Boulder with its steep cliffs and tree-carpeted valleys gripped her attention. As she sighed and gasped out her window Meme yawned. Nothing about America impressed my grandmother. "The Alps are so much nicer," she'd counter when my mother exclaimed how magnificent the mountains were. Yet, David and Ray were enthralled by the scenery. Pat and her children, Johnny and Joey, stared out the windows in amazement. Joe, with a pack of Pall Malls wrapped in the sleeve of his white t-shirt, negotiated the hills and turns like a pro. The Winnebago came to a stop at the Thompson Respirator Company just as my Marie's ears popped and her hearing was restored. A technician came out and tuned the respirator. He informed her that the demand for this type of respirator had been reduced and she should keep two on hand. Marie had outlived most of the polio patients that needed the Thompson Respirator to survive.

The plan from the beginning was to drive to California to visit the Youngson Family, who my parents had known in the army while stationed in England. This required returning north through Nevada towards the seemingly endless horizon. The first night on this route they stopped outside of Las Vegas. The heat of the day had made sleeping inside unbearable. David and Ray decided to sleep outside on the roof. The stars were bright and scattered. Soon they drifted off to sleep. At two in the morning they woke, shivering. They snuck quietly back into the Winnebago where the warmth of the day lingered. As they placed their sleeping bags behind Marie's rocking bed, their shivering subsided and they fell back asleep. Only an hour later, Ray felt a tugging at the bottom of his sleeping bag. He tried pulling it up only to have the fabric pulled violently out of his grasp. "Oh my God!" he yelled as he realized that the rocking bed's fan-belt had latched onto the sleeping bag and was swallowing it. Simultaneously, the rocking bed lurched and bucked, waking up Marie and everyone else. Pat ran and shut off the bed while David got the Thompson Respirator and chest-piece. David and Ray slowly untangled the fabric from the fan-belt. Once the sleeping bag was released, the travelers held their breath as Pat turned on the rocking bed. Even though it worked properly again, everyone was shaken. They all tried to go back to sleep, but only Joe and the children were successful.

The following day as the sun rose, an eerie light crept into the Winnebago. It framed the distant barren mountains in pink and orange. Pat woke up with the sun and remarked; "Naytcha is difrint every day out here." Marie replied, "You betcha!" She was fascinated by colloquialisms. The language of Ruth Avenue touched and tickled her. As much as she would admonish us for the use of a double negative, she'd hear Eddie Nelson say, "I didn't do nuthin!" and she would understand. For fun, my mother and I would practice saying the days of the week in the Pawtucket vernacular; "Mundy, Tewsdy, Wednsdy, and Frydeey," we'd chant. If she were sulking, I'd ask her what the day was. If her mood was vulnerable to humor she'd say, "Mondeee!" So when she called from Nevada to say that money was tight, I answered, "I tole you that you shouldn't have went thah!" "You nevah tole me nuthin like that eithah!" she interjected. I withdrew money and sent it to Western Union. Meme had sent for money from England, but it was delayed. When she asked me how things were going, I did not have the courage to describe the insanity of events after Patrick's party. Patrick's court appearance had resulted in a continuance and that guaranteed that my mother would eventually know. "Don't worry about nuthin, Ma," I said as I hung up the phone.

Nacimiento Road

Nacimiento Road connects Highway 1 to Highway 101, in the Salinas Valley below Big Sur and King City. During my time in the army, my friends and I would drive up the curving, thin dirt road and marvel at the steep grassy slopes plummeting only a few feet away, descending into a deep dale. There were no guardrails to prevent a plunge. At the summit of the drive there was a campground, amidst redwoods and oak trees.

My former roommate and friend, Roy Call, met my mother in Monterey and introduced her to my Fort Ord friends, who had worked the psychiatric ward with me. They shared a house on Prescott Avenue with tie-dyed curtains. Egg cartons were nailed onto the walls to accommodate the sound of the guitars, lutes, harmonicas, and singing that prevailed late into the night.

"Bernie told me that we had to go to Big Sur and Sand Dollar Beach," Marie enthused. "He sent us home movies, but he said that crossing Bixby Bridge and watching the Little Sur River crash against the ocean should only be viewed in person." Roy rubbed the corner of his moustache and pushed down his round, gold wire-rimmed spectacles on his nose, smiling bemusedly. Roy stood next to Marie's bed in the back of the bus. "Did he tell you about Nacimiento Road?" he asked. "No," she responded, with a gleam in her eye. Roy went on to describe the dirt road, its steep vistas and redwood trees. Marie was giddy with excitement. "It's settled then," she announced. "Nacimiento Road 'tis!" Meme looked at her daughter in horror. "Certainly, Marie, you mustn't believe that this lorry can negotiate a road like that!" My mother glanced at Roy. "We can do it. It will be exciting, and we'll take it slow," he reassured the crew.

As the Winnebago climbed Highway 68 out of Pacific Grove, brown kelp beds could be seen floating in the ocean. The air was bright and clear. Meme stood next to Roy, staring at the vast ocean. Crooked Monterey pines blocked the view of the summit. When Roy turned the Winnebago onto Highway 1, he looked in the rear view mirror. "There's Monterey Bay," he announced, as everyone ran to the back window to see the blue crescent of water, 1000 feet below. As they crossed the Carmel River, a large artichoke farm with a few dilapidated shacks on the perimeter caught my mother's attention. "Oh my! Are those migrant workers, Roy?" she asked. She strained to see boxes of artichokes being thrown onto conveyors by the people below, whose wide-brimmed straw hats ruffled in the morning breeze. "Perhaps they will make a better life here, someday." Roy drove Pooh past Carmel River Beach; waves exploded onto the hardened sand and the river met furiously with the ocean. After passing Point Lobos, they crossed Bixby Bridge; puffy clouds of fog were drifting through the tall pilings under the road. Marie relished the chronology of all the landmarks that I had described while I was stationed in California. "This is unbelievable!" she chirped. She looked at the crew and laughed. "Naytcha!" she sighed playfully. They stopped for lunch at Hurricane Point, braving the wind to get a view of Monterey to the north and Big Sur to the south. Everyone but Marie looked over the edge of the steep cliff. They listened to the barking of seals and pointed to three or four wrecked cars strewn in the brush on the slope.

Roy advised Marie that they would need to hurry, as Nacimiento Road should not be negotiated in the dark. In Big Sur, huge redwoods formed a canopied tunnel and the Little Sur River rushed across a grassy meadow. Highway 1, carved into the side of the coastal mountain range, challenged Pooh with hairpin turns and sudden stops. Roy pulled into the large lot above Sand Dollar beach. Pat stayed with my mother as the crew scoured the beach for fragile sand dollars. Tea and crackers were prepared as the crew scampered up the sand dunes with their shells. The sun began to descend into the ocean as Roy swiveled in the driver's seat and asked, "Ready?" Marie felt like she had just handed her ticket to a rollercoaster operator and was walking the creaky boards to the gate.

Nacimiento Road is very steep initially, and the respirator and the battery both had to be secured. Pooh strained slowly around curves only a few feet away from a steep pitch into the valley. Everyone became silent, exhilarated by the view and the challenge. The Winnebago had to stop several times and back up carefully to facilitate a turn or to let an approaching vehicle pass. Motorists gawked as the behemoth bus trekked slowly up the road. Roy gripped the steering wheel confidently even as his passengers gaped at the cliffs in awe. The eight-track tape stopped playing, but no one noticed. Pat, Ray, and David clung to my mother's mattress, guarding against any sudden shifts. The Pacific Ocean glimmered like a planet to the west until a wide bend revealed the summit and campground. Smiles of relief and enthusiastic chatter commenced. When they pulled into the campsite, Roy turned in the driver's seat. He had driven this road many times and the joy etched on Marie's face made him smile. Spontaneously, the crew began to clap. Roy stood and bowed. "I never doubted you for a second, Roy!" Marie laughed.

Pooh eventually journeyed north on Highway 101, to return to San Francisco. All the passengers re-lived their adventure to each other as they headed east to Meadville, Pennsylvania. Grandma Mulligan, Sister James Francis, Uncle Joe, Uncle Ed, Aunt Audrey, the cousins, and many old acquaintances anticipated the arrival of the curious family bus. The Meadville Tribune had written a front page story about the Winnebago procured with green stamps. Meme and Marie smiled as Ray and David repeatedly described the precipice that lurked only inches from the window as they navigated the winding, treacherous Nacimiento Road.

The four days of travel to Meadville were dreamy and quiet. The landscape's diversity mesmerized the crew and passengers. Games of cards and scrabble mixed with desultory conversation at the campsites in the evening. My mother was relatively happy but distracted. One evening as the Mississippi River sparkled red and silver she composed a poem:

B.J.M.

Life dealt him such a hand
You'd say,
He should have passed,
Thrown in his cards-
Called a misdeal, perhaps-
But that was not his way:
He kept his fate
And played it to the end

Her guilt and longing forced her to close her eyes and spiritually depart from the tranquil ride. "What I would give to slam a door or a telephone receiver," she thought. She pretended to sleep. The whining of the tires on the road, constant and mantra-like soothed the guilt and afforded acuity of thought. Without embarrassment she tried to conjure her dead husband. "Why aren't you here?" she pondered.

Arriving in Meadville as a celebrity did not alter her preoccupation with her husband. On the day that the Winnebago was parked at Arch Street, Grandma and Sister affectionately tapped her lifeless hands and she smiled and conversed. Even the chaos of running children and the endless convoy of supplies could not shake her resolve to commune spiritually with her husband. Falling asleep the night of her arrival, she imagined that she'd awake to his gentle touch in the morning. Instead she awoke alone. She felt vaguely content in her mourning, as if her desire to be with him was resolve in itself. Marie ruminated as blue dawn light crept towards her bed.

In Meadville, Bernard inhabits every scene that comes into view. What I imagine to be his childhood memories animate each moment in my mind. When I awake at dawn, the noise of morning deliveries, the slamming of doors, and the squeaking of brakes roll up the hill to Arch Street from downtown; I see him as a boy in this house, rousing to the familiar work-song of morning. He rubs his eyes and reaches for his glasses before sliding his legs lithely from under the covers. He runs down the stairs to a stack of wheat pancakes piled on a plate. The heat of the cast iron stove emanates from the door of the kitchen into the dining room. I inhale the hopeful joy of being an 11-year-old boy in Western Pennsylvania, surrounded by persistent rivers, verdant trees, and beckoning hills.

I have been sitting here for hours, seeing things as perhaps he once did. I am looking at the cement block porch with its smooth grey finish, admiring it as a castle. It was the Alamo for him and his brothers, and a monastery for his sister. Yet, the stateliness of the porch's fortress is betrayed by the peeling, wooden edifice that surrounds it. In my stillness, I am a captive audience to the life that pervades all things, even stone and siding.

A fly buzzes stuck between the screen and the glass of the window behind me. I sense the desperation of the poor fly trapped in that small place. The sun will rise and the heat will suffocate him slowly within the steamy confines of the window.

I close my eyes and see Bernard again, but as a young man now. He hits the baseball squarely and his long sleeved shirt ruffles around his taut young muscles. He runs ambitiously towards first base as the ball he has hit sails over the shortstop's glove and skids past the left fielder all the way to the fence. His glasses jump rhythmically on the bridge of his nose as he sprints. His tongue hangs out slightly from the corner of his mouth and he strains every part of his anatomy striving for second base. He is completely committed. His lungs fill with air as he stands on second base, the sun shining on him like a spotlight.

Bernard, your life, with its victories and defeats, imbued your character with strength and resolve. My story is yours, because you gave your life to me as a husband and a friend. Meadville molded you. Your laughter, your language, and your moral strength were and are the foundation of my life. One slight shift in your existence would have changed our lives. Had I not met you, the best and worst of life would not have been mine to discover.

Chapter Thirty-Nine - Feats of Daring

Young Marie with her camera

Michael's voice could be heard anywhere in the house. Concerned about Patrick's party and the mess with the police, he spoke with Marie in a harried tone. Patrick had been charged with disturbing the peace. As I stood at the top of the stairs, I could overhear the conversation. Michael believed that if our father were alive, the consequences would have been too great for Patrick to ever behave this badly. He fumed that I am indifferent to his behavior, and that she coddled Patrick similarly to the cats and the neighbors' children. Marie's quieter tone was forlorn and hurt; she expressed that she always did the best she could manage; Patrick was so distant now —it wasn't as if she could chase him down. As the room grew silent Marie closed her eyes. There was a time when she felt physically strong. A memory came to her; soothing her frayed nerves and offering an escape from the turmoil.

Marie pushed the sheets aside as she eagerly grabbed her nightshirt. It was June 21st, 1928—her 10th birthday, and her father was home! She scampered down the stairs, swinging from the base of the thick bannister past the grandfather clock and into the sun drenched dining room. Her mother and father stood behind their chairs in anticipation of her arrival. "Happy Birthday, Marie," they chimed in unison.

A box wrapped in gold paper sat on the table. The ribbon adorning the top of the gift sparkled in the morning sun. "Go ahead," her father smiled. "Open it!" Marie meticulously scratched at the tape until the paper, untorn, was pushed aside. She opened the box carefully, and felt a heavy object inside the crepe paper. She saw a reflection of herself in the lens as she pulled out a camera. "Oh Papa! Oh Meme!" she squealed. A folded tripod was leaning in the corner. Marie put down the camera and glanced into the bottom of the box to make sure it was empty. She ran to her parents and hugged them tightly.

Marie had already spent hours with her father in his dark room, watching the mystical process of capturing time. With a camera of her own, and a thorough tutorial by her father on how to use it, Marie ventured out into the enormous backyard. The soaring pines, the flowering apple and pear trees, and the old English walls became her stage. The timer and tripod allowed her to photograph herself. She was the star of this show. Marie photographed herself performing many feats of athleticism and courage. She jumped the fence, running the length of the back walk at full speed. She balanced on the high wall above the garden. She climbed trees and made stoic expressions. Her final feat was a challenge in photography as well as physical daring. She tied the clothesline between two poles, each four feet off the ground. She had to time her jump at the exact second that the shutter clicked. Marie performed the act over and over until she was exhausted.

After dinner she went into the basement darkroom to process her film. She was pleased with the results. One shot was perfect; she flew over the clothesline with aplomb. Once it was dry, she glued the picture onto the front of her scrapbook. She pressed her white ink pen into the stiff black paper to caption underneath the photo: **Made it.**

Chapter Forty - Lunch with Meme

Alfredo's Restaurant, Providence, RI

"Let's go, Meme!" I yelled from the kitchen table where Kathy and I sat. Rick Derringer blasted Chuck Berry's guitar licks from Patrick's room. Brandy, the family's St. Bernard, sat by my feet, drooling on the floor. Pat was cooking lunch for her children, who were playing in the backyard. Kathy Mitchell, teasingly called "Mitch", had recently been hired to care for my mother full-time if Pat or I were away. For now, she worked in the afternoon, four days a week. She was feeding my mother as Ray the mailman sat in the easy chair beside them, chatting and drinking the coffee Kathy had made for him. "Where are you going?" Pat asked; she banged a macaroni and cheese-laden wooden spoon on a pan. "Meme is taking us out for lunch," Kathy responded enthusiastically.

Meme emerged from the bathroom smiling, a colorful scarf draped over one shoulder. "I am ready," she announced. The three of us got in my red VW station-wagon and drove down Ruth Avenue towards the East Side of Providence. I stopped in a carwash on Pawtucket Avenue. As our front wheels were grasped to guide us through, Meme remarked, "I've never been in a a carwash before!" When the separate workstations sprayed, slapped, or brushed the car, Meme sat mesmerized. "This IS fun," she exclaimed as we were entering the large, noisy blower. "I'd like to do this again." She was gleaming in the back seat. "America," she laughed, "so much water down the drain."

Kathy and I had attempted to find a restaurant that might appeal to her palate. It was difficult. Once we drove all the way to Galilee to George's Restaurant, considered by many to be the best in Rhode Island. "They put artificial bread crumbs and crude seasonings on perfectly good fish," she commented afterwards. Kathy had previously been a waitress at Alfredo's on Thayer Street, near Brown University, and knew they cooked well. In an effort to placate Meme, she arranged for a meal of homemade pasta and a light wine sauce. As the maitre d' ushered us into our seats, a bottle of Pinot Noir was brought over for her inspection. Meme smiled graciously and nodded.

We waited for our food to arrive and discussed movies, the news, and my mother. She looked out the window at the Brown students as they scurried by. Her reflection in the window offered me a view, although hazy, of the other side of her face. Her eyebrows twitched. I could see she was grappling with the words she had chosen for this meeting. Meme moved her wine glass like a chess-piece towards me. As I poured her more wine, she asked, "What will she do when I am gone?" Meme's voice quivered as she sat back in her chair. "I will take care of her," I answered quickly. "After all, she chose me. Don't worry Meme." She blinked back her tears and looked out the window. I prayed that my words could ease her mind. "I am tired," she said. "I am returning to Bournemouth and I don't think I will be back."

Bernie, David, Patrick and Meme

In 1973, Meme returned to England. She was exhausted and craved the soothing comfort of her garden, the quiet of her home, and the blissfully slow pace of life in Bournemouth. Relieved that Marie's care had been secured, she could delight in the sound of the grandfather clock and the melody of the birds feeding outside her window. Meme accepted that she would not see her daughter again. Crossword puzzles, afternoon tea, and restful sleep were her priorities now. She had seen the worst of humanity: two world wars, the great depression, famine, polio, and heartache. She counted American food among those atrocities. In the prior two decades, she had crossed the Atlantic frequently, staying at Ruth Avenue for months or years to care for us, sacrificing her idyllic life in England to attend to our needs. After her departure, Meme wrote often, and my mother received each letter with anticipation and delight. Marie's brother Maurice had Parkinson's disease, and Meme would explain to her the latest developments and describe the treatments. They talked on the phone periodically, and sometimes I would pick up the line, finding solace in their conversation. On these mornings, I would emerge from the basement to the wondrous music of my mother speaking in French.

Chapter Forty-One - Departure

"I stuck my key into the car door and it broke..."

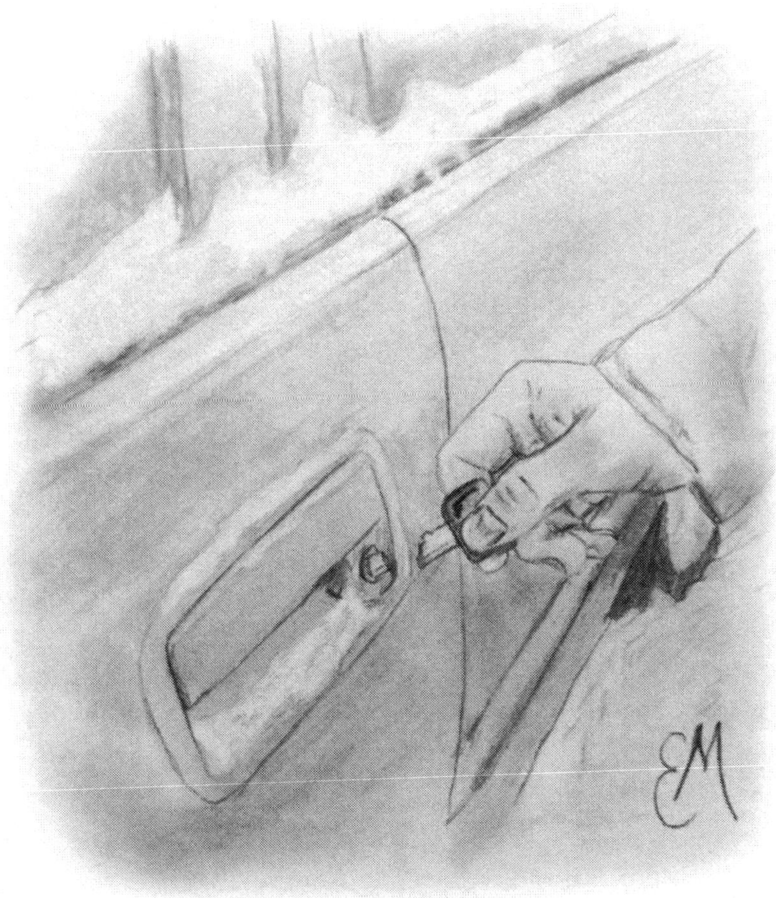

Bernie's Volvo

At my mother's gentle insistence, Kathy and I moved out of the house and into a third story loft on the East Side of Providence. Pat Kralik and her children permanently filled the space we left at 56 Ruth Avenue. The new arrangement was a positive solution to the question of my mother's health, and Kathy and I finally felt confident in pursuing our dream of living in Monterey, California. Tom Rush had just covered Joni Mitchell's song *Urge for Going* at the time, and we would play that song from the jukebox every time that we sat for a meal at Spat's Restaurant, fantasizing about our escape. That winter, Rhode Island experienced a particularly severe ice storm. I had purchased a 1967 Volvo 122S. On the morning after the storm, I crunched my way out to my car and noticed that the tire was flat and encased in ice. I stuck my key into the car door and it broke, leaving half a key in my hand and the balance wedged in the lock. I went back up the three flights of stairs and sat on our bed, where Kathy was sleeping. She propped herself up on one elbow and yawned, "What's the matter?" "We have to get out of here!" I implored.

Patrick, David, Pat Kralik, Ann Regan, Susan DeSorcy, and Kathy Mitchell were all capable of caring for my mother, and although I was happy at the prospect of starting my life anew, it was sad to leave her and the home that held so many memories. I put *Abbey Road* by the Beatles on the turntable as I washed and cared for her. A sense of guilt clouded the serenity of the moment. "Can I call you if things don't work out," she asked. "Of course," I replied smiling. Kathy and I loaded up the Volvo and left Rhode Island in August with a bold plan to visit our many friends scattered across the United States. Our first stop was Washington, DC. Strangely, we had arrived on the day that Nixon resigned as president.

That night, during our phone conversation the historic event dominated my discussion, but as always she was lost in the swirling daily excitement of Ruth Avenue. "Ma, this is big," I lectured. "This is History." During our conversation, someone returned from the grocery store and was holding items up in the mirror for distribution. "Cupboard seven," she instructed. "Well, Bernie," she laughed.

"Chamberlain, Churchill, Stalin, Hitler, and Mussolini made history, didn't they?" There was another pause in our conversation as she announced instructions. Returning to my point, she replied, "Nixon has scarred the political scene for a good while now." There was another pause. "Cupboard eight behind the cereal," she advised. "Ma," I asked, "Are you sober?" "Well, not quite, but I only had a little."

My mother's indulgences were a source of consternation for some. She had always pushed the boundaries of her corporeal limitations by mental stimulation, and scotch and the infrequent joint were instruments for toying with reality. The exhausting effort of fantasy that she had experienced while encased in an iron lung day after day was not entirely gone. She spent long periods of time locked in place. If she invited me to look out the window at a cloud or if she was crying while listening to Brahms, clearly she was affected. She loved being mischievous; she loved the reversal of our roles when a vice was involved. How had she managed to discover such joy in her life? I never felt compelled to take one moment away from her.

"Susan is going to be driving me to Niagara Falls in the Winnebago next week!" my mother exclaimed during one of my calls home. "Ma, she just got her license last week," I warned. "She takes such good care of me," she rebutted. "She's so responsible." "She is only sixteen," I said in exasperation. "I suppose it would be better for me to just stay here and read safe and sound," she added sarcastically. Eventually my protests would prove futile and in the end I would simply wish her well on her travels.

On our journey across the country, my plan was to call her once a week. She was hardly ever there. She was off in the Winnebago, traveling to Meadville, Lido's Beach, or the White Mountains in New Hampshire. Sometimes she would have the teenagers drive all the way to the L&M motel in Schenectady, New York, just to socialize with the Martins. By the time Kathy and I found our home in California, my mother decided that telephone communication could be reduced to once every two weeks. These calls could go on for hours. We would discuss new albums that had come out or new books that we felt were relevant to read. Whenever I would ask her how things were going, she would always reply, "delightful." Ruth Avenue was becoming more of a social hub than ever. The teenagers were growing up and perhaps putting some distance between themselves and their own parents. Traveling with Marie was an adventure. The trust that my mother placed in these young people bolstered their self-confidence. There would be the echo of laughter in the background during the calls home. Most times, upon hanging up the phone, I felt a strong urge to return to Rhode Island. I missed Ruth Avenue and my mother.

Chapter Forty-Two - Salt in the Wound

"...she was uncompromising with anyone's desire that she embrace the Deity who had treated her daughter so harshly."

Meme in Bournemouth

In 1975, Andree Cooper entered the hospital, refusing the treatment of doctors and the visitation of clergy; she was uncompromising with anyone's desire that she embrace the Deity who had treated her daughter so harshly. Three weeks after her admission, she died peacefully. At that time, I realized what a critical part Meme had played in our existence and mine in particular. I reminisced with Kathy about Meme, how she bathed us by pouring water out of a saucepan on our heads in the tub, making us giggle; how she would slip us an extra dollar if we performed a task well. Without her, my mother, my father, and we four children would not have survived as a family unit. Whenever there was a gap in our care, or if there was a financial crisis, Meme would respond quickly.

When my mother called me with the news she was sobbing. "Do you want me to come home for a while?" I asked. She refused. "Once again, I can't be there. Once again I have to mourn here and not in England where I belong," she lamented. I just sat on the floor with the phone to my ear listening to her cry. I tried to console her, but she needed to weep. Meme had been her strength. The secrets they shared in French would now just be an echo in my mother's memory. The cruelty of her paralysis reprised its role as the salt in her wound. "I'm tired, Bernie," she said weakly. I asked her to call me the following day. She did. In fact, she called me every day for a week. I sat on the floor again each time as she wailed. "I'm so sorry, Mom, so sorry."

Surrounded by children, adults, cats, and dogs, Marie eventually persevered. Fifty-six Ruth Avenue was so alive that surrender to the doldrums was impossible. Each conversation, touch, and smile provided light and offered hope for survival without Meme. In time, her calls to me slowed and her mood brightened. She started to talk about a bold plan to drive across Canada and then south down the Pacific Coast until she reached our house, where she could stay as long as she wanted.

Chapter Forty-Three - The Inheritance

Marie with Pat's daughter, Heather

Meme died an English citizen with valuable property in Paris and heirs in the United States and England. Governments, lawyers, and landlords plundered her estate. Still, my mother received an $88,000 disbursement. Suddenly, money was no longer a concern of hers. Marie installed wall-to-wall carpeting and purchased a new stereo as well as a grand piano for Patrick; his playing gave her immense joy. She finalized her ambitious travel plan: a four month odyssey through Canada to Vancouver and down the coast of the US to Monterey. After a three week rest in Monterey, they would journey to Wisconsin to visit a friend and back to Rhode Island.

Kathy and I lived in Pacific Grove with several roommates. There was one bathroom, one kitchen, and one phone. Kathy had organized a study routine that would take place with a student from her biology class over the phone, and they could sometimes talk for hours. My calls from home were also long, due to their animated nature. On one particular night, my call from my mother conflicted with one of Kathy's phone-study sessions.

The phone rang. I picked the receiver gently off the cradle and answered, "Deis bonus." "Bernie? Is that you?" "Yeah, Ma, I'm sorry, but my friends and I are trying to communicate in Latin. Everything I know is from the Mass." "Your Father would be either really angry or really proud," she laughed. "Kathy thinks it's dumb," I told her. "For once, I agree with her," my mother answered. She went over the roster, timetable, and route of the impending trip. Meanwhile, I realized that I was encroaching upon Kathy's imminent call, but could not stop my mother. "Sal will be the principal driver. His band is drifting apart and he's in the mood to explore," she announced. Cindy Desorcy, Bill Hanson, Ann Regan, Doreen Guy, Margaret Rook (my wife's little sister), Stephan Gentile, and Alisha all were going to be on board. I was relieved that Ann was going to be on the trip. My mother depended on her, and although she was the least subtle person I had ever met, she was an excellent caretaker. Cindy would be good company for Marie; she read books incessantly and spoke intelligently. Bill Hanson was perpetually happy and exuberant.

Stephan Gentile would offer comic relief, and Alisha loved to write for Marie and had wonderful penmanship. Doreen and Margaret were in their early teens and this trip would be a huge geography lesson for them. I could imagine my mother's narration, "Do you see that, girls? That's the Mississippi River. You should read Mark Twain's *Huckleberry Finn*."

My mother stayed on the phone for over an hour. Anyone trying to reach Kathy or any of the occupants of the house received only a busy signal. Kathy spent a significant amount of time in the kitchen banging pots and pans loudly. She walked by the phone periodically, glaring at me. This intrusion was only foreshadowing the much larger inconvenience to come. Perhaps, Kathy had forgotten the impact my mother and the gang could have on one's living situation, or maybe she was in denial. Neither one of us understood the fissure that was forming between us. She dreaded the impending visit, but I found it hard to mask my joy.

Chapter Forty-Four - Home

Michael, Kellie, Phyllis, and Stacie Mulligan

My brother Michael and his wife Phyllis had two children, Kellie and Stacie. Michael had purchased a house on Frederick Street, a couple of blocks away from Ruth Avenue. When my mother called me, she would often report about Michael and his family. All of our relationships became more comfortable with time. Patrick took on more responsibility for the care of his mother. He played piano for her, which she greatly enjoyed. With his left hand floating and diving over the keys, he would compose and deliver complex melodies. His exquisite touch and bold chord changes, filled with emotion, expressed the feelings he could not verbalize. David found a girlfriend. He filled his book with beautiful poems and listened to bands like *Strawbs* and *Blondel*. He, too, cared affectionately for our mother.

In the spring of 1975, I came home from California during a break from college. I stayed at Ruth Avenue, sleeping in the basement on an army cot a few feet away from the litter box. All during the night, cats traipsed over me, inspecting and evaluating the significance of my station in the household dynamic. I rarely spoke to my brothers. I couldn't find them amongst Pat Kralik, her five children, the Kathy's, and the kaleidoscope of my mother's ever-expanding adopted family. My mother's room had remained corporate headquarters for the neighborhood's youths long after the green stamp drive ceased operation.

On the first morning, I charged up the stairs in my bare feet as the house came to life. The new wall-to-wall carpeting cushioned my step until, suddenly, I felt a puddle of cold slime underfoot. One of the girls caught my chagrined look and laughingly advised me about the minefield of drool strategically hidden in the carpeting by Brandy. "Yuck!" I groaned.

Susan Desorcy was already standing on the sideboard of the rocking bed, perusing a catalog with my mother. Pat's children were seated around the kitchen table as Pat worked the stove. Sal came in through the front door, having spent the night in the Winnebago with Bill, Cindy, and Alisha. The kettle was boiling and there were four cats on the counter slurping cat food. I listened as the buzz of the chaos mingled with sound of Carole King's *So Far Away.* I sat in the easy chair in my mother's room and someone put a cup of coffee on the armrest for me.

"Don't I get a kiss?" my mother inquired. "I didn't want to interrupt your study of the Sears product line," I responded. As I sipped my coffee, I observed in amusement a parade of young people who came and went, each reporting outcomes or receiving instructions. My mother had a specific purpose for each young person that came to our home. It seemed as if I had been politely urged to go find my own way in the world, perhaps because I had been exerting authority which conflicted with my mother's ambitions. I felt relief that my responsibility for my mother's care had been lifted from me. Patrick and David's issues were no longer mine. Still, I was hurt by my exclusion. In an attempt to reconnect with her, I insisted on spending as much time as possible with her on my last day in Rhode Island.

"Ma, there's a new record out by Crosby and Nash. The first song is about the plight of the whales. James Taylor is singing with them. Do you want to listen?" "I'd love to," she beamed. A powerful three-part harmony started the album off and she yelled at me from under the headphones, "This is fantastic!" I gazed at her as she closed her eyes and let the song flood her senses. Suddenly, I felt silly for my periodic embarrassment about my mother and her spectacular life. The older I became, the more I began to fully appreciate her incredible tenacity for living. Her eyes remained closed as she listened and I scanned the distance between us. Before I left, I kissed her goodbye. "I miss you, Ma," I said smiling. "I miss you too," she responded as she spied one of her minions in the front yard. "Here comes... Safe travels, Bernie. Please call me when you get back to California".

Chapter Forty-Five - Pacific Grove

"How is this going to play out?"

509 Tenth Street, Pacific Grove, California

The house on 509 Tenth Street in Pacific Grove was narrow with high ceilings. Artichoke plants protruded from the sandy soil around the base of the house. We had one garden where we grew only strawberries and another with our favorite vegetables. Kathy and I had achieved a level of peace. We both realized that my mother's visit would alter the harmony by injecting logistical hurdles and emotional issues into our home, not to mention polluting the local vernacular with the verbal eccentricities of so many Rhode Islanders. First, there was the problem of where to park the Winnebago. Our street was more of an alley than a road, so Kathy and I were concerned about the RV and where it would fit. Kathy felt obligated to warn the neighbors and the landlady about the impending visit of my mother and her entourage. Words could not prepare them for my mother's impact, and the equally startling sideshows of the roaring vehicle and boisterous teenagers. Still I made the rounds and attempted to brace everyone for the arrival. "Errrr... My mother is paralyzed and she has to have a portable respirator to breathe. She received a Winnebago from the collection of Green Stamps. She'll be parked here for three weeks along with the eight teenagers who are caring for her." The neighbors and landlady just scrunched their brows in puzzled bemusement. "That's incredible," our landlady retorted. "Quite a wonderful story," my next door neighbor commented. "They will know soon enough," I thought.

Kathy was crying on our bed when the Winnebago lumbered slowly up our street. She was fretting. "How is this going to play out?" she asked. To me, it was like diving into the deep end of a cold river. If I thought about it too much, I'd be a nervous wreck. I had grown up with the antics of my family, our friends, and the small zoo of animals. I understood that the Mulligan family could not be discreet even if we tried.

We decided to park the mobile home on the sidewalk so that the door of the Winnebago lined up to the steps to the front door of the house. When they arrived, I ran down our steps and jumped through the door. I stepped on the sideboard of the rocking bed and kissed my mother. Most of the occupants just seemed happy to be in one place for an extended period of time. "Are you going to play guitar for me?" Marie smiled.

That night, I invited my friend Rick over to accompany me and join in the experience. Everyone laughed and sang. All my friends came over that evening. I searched their demeanor as they beheld this beaming paralyzed woman before them. The unfettered joy surrounding my mother dampened any apprehension my new friends, who had never met her, may have had. Too soon the guitars were tucked away, as my mother fought against her need to sleep. As the eight occupants of the Winnebago and the five residents of the house found beds, I asked my mother if I could get her ready for the night. As I gave her the usual medications, holding a glass of water with a straw, I noticed a new small pill. I walked behind her bed to place the medicine in the cupboard and read the label. I held my breath. It was morphine. I decided not to inquire because she was tired and happy. "Good night, Ma" I said. "Sweet dreams."

I skipped up the stairs and back into the house. I found Sal sitting at the kitchen table with a cup of tea. He had been the principal driver. Exhaustion and relief was etched on his face. I asked him how the trip had gone, thus far. He shook his head and laughed slightly. "Insane," he said.

"Your mother insisted that we drive up Mount Rainier to the visitor's station. As we approached the last hill before the visitor's center, I smelled burning liquid. I couldn't shift the gears. The transmission had over heated and I couldn't turn it around so I had to drive the beast backwards for three miles. Motorists driving up were absolutely freaked out when they saw us coming at them. Finally, I managed to turn the face of the Winnebago around and glide to a gas station at the bottom of the mountain."

(A Cartoon by Sal)

I heated some tea while Sal described waking up to mosquito covered windows in the morning in Arcadia and seeing the Rocky Mountains for the first time. He made it clear that they all were having fun. "Oh yeah," Sal giggled. "When we were in Vancouver, Cindy, Stephan, and Bill went into the City. They knew where we going to be camped so they agreed to meet up with us later. When we got to the campsite it was full, on account that we didn't call ahead. We found another campsite, but didn't realize that we hadn't informed Cindy, Stephan, and Bill where we were, and what THAT meant. Once we realized that they couldn't find us, the campsite owners told them that we had left to find another place. They were absolutely bummed. They moped and wandered off looking for a place to stay warm and get out of the fog. In the morning we went into Vancouver and put an All-Points Bulletin out for them. Later that morning, they turned up at the police station having slept miserably in a damp, cold, deserted gas station."

Even though he was animated in his descriptions of their

escapades, I could see that his nerves were shot. He was twitching. Finally in exasperation he said, "I had no idea that it was going to be like this." "Are you sorry that you made the trip?" I asked defensively. "Absolutely not!" he laughed, "It's nice to be here, sitting and drinking tea and relaxing. I'll admit. Still, I'll let your mother tell you about the biggest adventure." Perhaps, understanding that I found the stories disturbing, Sal spared me some of the details. The next day I caught my mother gazing out the window at the fog, as it filtered through the Monterey pine tree in front of our neighbor's yard. She turned to me as I sat in the driver's seat examining the eight-track cassettes in a milk carton on the floor. "I had quite a fright in Washington State, Bernie." As the words came out, I could see that she was still shaken. "I was so frightened," she stammered. "It has affected my dreams. I had insisted that we drive onto the beach. We opened all the windows and the sound of the waves and the smell of the ocean felt exhilarating. When we parked I stared at the horizon as sea birds fought the wind. It was so lovely. Cindy began to feel anxious about the tide coming in. 'Just another minute,' I said. Still, when the water started to reach the front tires before retreating I began to feel uneasy. I gave the signal to leave. Sal put Pooh in gear, but we could not get out of the wet sand. I closed my eyes and prayed, but it was as if I was at the pool at Chapin. I could not get that feeling of being lowered into the water out of my head. I could read the anxiety on everyone's face. They had trucks tying ropes and chains attempting to free us from the advancing water but nothing worked." My mother stopped and began to cry. I walked over with some Kleenex and wiped her eyes. I placed my hand on hers. "My mouth was so dry that I couldn't speak," she continued as her tears slowed. "We had contacted the police and they dispatched a truck large enough to do the job. The tires made a sucking sound as we were pulled out. By this time the water was up to the stairs and I could feel the waves slapping the front of Pooh."

I stayed with her until she drifted off to sleep. I had no intention of lecturing her. She would continue to challenge the predicament of her paralysis no matter what I said. I was twenty six years old now.

The fantastic nature of her extraordinary existence awed me all the more as I matured. When she told me that she had just about exhausted her money I was not surprised or disappointed. I was proud of her. She grasped every second of life reveling in her own vulnerability. Marie Andree Cooper, how could I ever fear for you? I could never be so arrogant as to question your judgment. How could anyone?

Chapter Forty-Six - The Karass Takes Over

California Coast South of Monterey

I gazed out the bay window at the Winnebago, amused by the neighborhood's general consternation over my mother's presence. Kathy was beginning to adjust, but was doing so by spending more and more time at school in the library and student union. Kathy and I had made pasta with clam sauce for thirteen people the night before, and we consumed almost as many bottles of wine. We had been singing a raucous version of *Its All Over Now,* by the Rolling Stones, at one-thirty in the morning. The Pacific Grove Police fielded a complaint from one of our neighbors and they had politely requested that we tone it down. A cop knocked on the door in the middle of a drunken chorus. "Who's in charge here?" he asked, smiling. I put my guitar down and headed outside, replying, "I am." "Well, tell your friends that IT IS ALL OVER NOW!" he roared, barely concealing his delight over his cleverness.

After he left, the door of the motor-home burst open. One of the teenagers jumped out onto the curb and got sick. She sat for a moment on the sidewalk before retreating back inside. I decided to see if Ma was still awake. I ambled quietly out and peered through her window. "Come on in," my mother whispered. I shut her rocking bed off and secured her chest-piece expertly before plugging the hose in. As I cranked her bed into its familiar 'S' configuration, Ma winked; "How's Kathy holding up?" "I'll probably get some grief about the police and she'll want me to apologize to the neighbors after you leave. This is not Ruth Avenue, you know," I noted as I placed her glasses on. I set the kettle on for tea before nonchalantly asking, "What's the morphine for, Ma?" "Kidney stones, they are simply awful," she grimaced. As I set her cup holder on the pillows, she studied me intently. "Would you help me kill myself if I asked you?" she asked, earnestly. I pondered the question in silence, though not entirely shocked. "I don't know, Ma, I mean, I haven't really ever thought about it," I lied uncomfortably. She had casually invited me to "just put her out of her misery" more than once, and I was not unfamiliar with the quandary. The phrasing, tone, and setting for this particular query indicated that she had been thinking about it more seriously. It wasn't just an emotional outpouring of sorrow. My mother let the question go unanswered, although she had deftly planted a disconcerting seed in my brain.

We had both been reading "Cat's Cradle" by Kurt Vonnegut, and I assumed that Vonnegut's themes of life's meaning, death's inevitability, and the exploration of the roles people played in each other's lives had produced the question. My mother had been dreaming again of meeting Dad on the beach in Bournemouth. No one could fill the void left by the loss of her mother and her husband. The book stimulated fresh evaluation of her life and the many people she had come to depend on. The young adults who cared for her offered distraction and affection, which she relished, but these were no substitute for the private loves of her life. The term *karass* in "Cat's Cradle" refers to human contacts whose lives intertwine with each other, unconsciously helping one another accomplish life's tasks. My mother's relationship with the teenagers of Ruth Avenue fit that definition very well.

On the other hand, my mother's relationship with me was too complex to be completely defined. We would sometimes push each other gently away, only to later feel the pain of absence with remorse. During these times, in a panic, one of us would get on the phone. "Do you need me to come home, Ma?" I would ask. "No, Bernie, but you would if I needed you, wouldn't you?" she'd say. I often thought to myself, what if I *truly* needed to come home? As long as I remained away from her, my father's expectation that I would care for her loomed in my mind. My mother and I were both anguished over our responsibility for Michael's Vietnam experience. Did I fit the definition of *karass?* Perhaps, I was just a casual cog in her great machine? "You are more important to me than that," Marie would explain.

I retrieved the book-holder and opened "Cat's Cradle" at the bookmark. Tucking the pages under the wooden swivels I placed the contraption on her lap. She began to move the pages with her rubber tipped mouthpiece. From the driver's seat, I viewed Monterey Bay. Streaks of silver from the sky's reflection blended with brown from the kelp beds across the waves. My mind would not settle down even under the spell of soothing Pacific Ocean air. I pulled out my journal, sensing that the act of writing might cease the racing thoughts and flight of emotion I was experiencing.

I miss the chaos, the unending activity of cats and dogs, the intruding of humans, the teenagers and their laughter. There is no need to think or analyze when it is so busy. One needs only to respond. It is so peaceful here in Pacific Grove....

"Bernie!" Marie choked as she let the mouth-piece tumble off her bed and onto the floor. "What's the matter?" I asked. My mother's respirator had stopped and she was gasping. I ran to her bedside, yanked out the hose, checked for wires and turned the rocking bed on. It didn't work. "Hold on, Ma, we're not getting any voltage you must have been on battery all this time." The electrical cord from the house had been run through an open window. I scurried into the house following the cord. The plug lay on the floor just under the wall socket. Jamming the plug into the socket I relaxed. Unfortunately, I did not consider that the book-holder was still on my mother's lap and the rocking bed was on until I came through the Winnebago door. The book-holder was dancing around my mother's legs as if it were alive. By the time I stopped the bed, my mother's shins were bruised and bleeding. As I tended to her wounds, my mother lamented, "I am a slave to these bloody machines." "I am so sorry, Ma. I'll admit you couldn't breathe without them."

Having dealt with another crisis, reflection on the incident rendered us silent for a moment. I returned to the driver's seat with my twelve string guitar. Swiveling around to face my mother, smiling broadly, I smiled and exclaimed, "That WAS invigorating!" Ma nodded in agreement. "I want to write a poem," she announced. "Let's write a song instead, Ma," I said.

As I played a chord progression over and over, we worked the lyrics. After a few hours, we had completed our one and only joint musical composition. It is a love song to the Thompson Respirator:

I couldn't breathe without you/ I won't live without you
Thompson Machine mechanical dream
I know it's so hard to know what I mean
Mechanical Queen

Causing a scene about you
Mechanical dreams they're without you
Thompson Machine mechanical queen
I know it's so hard to know what I mean

I can't breathe without you/ I won't live without you
Thompson Machine mechanical queen
I know it's so hard to know what I mean
Mechanical Queen

Chapter Forty-Seven - Wish You Were Here

Winnebago stuck on the beach

On the day that she left, my mother and her *karass* coasted down 10th street into a bright blue sky and towards the ocean. All the excitement of the unanticipated daily events she and her crew provided were gone. My world resumed its motion. A relentless tide of term papers, guitar playing, and exploration of the Los Padres Forest closed over her wake. Yet, a guilt-ridden relief consumed me. My role as her last resort, that if all else fails she would inevitably "call Bernie," irked me. My lack of relevance to her left me feeling vacant, particularly in the context that my assistance was always assumed to be boundless and unquestioning. Watching the back of the bus as it disappeared, I realized that no matter how near or far the circus of Ruth Avenue might be, I would always be part of it. Dunkin Donuts' styrofoam cups strewn in the gutters of East Providence had always seemed more like real life to me than the spitting of whales on the Pacific horizon. As my life became more perfect, I began to feel like a failure. Was I truly living, or simply escaping? Even if I was only dreaming, my diaries were still filled with notes on my phone conversations with my mother. They were my only insights into her life at that time, and a testament to how important she was to me, regardless of the times when our relationship could be uncomfortable or disturbing.

"I wish you were here," she remarked on her telephone call from Wisconsin. "They were laying hands on me, hoping that these muscles would respond to begging the Lord for forgiveness." I slumped to the floor with my back against the wall, as the coiled telephone wire vibrated. "Did it work?" I asked, facetiously. "No, not yet, anyway," she laughed.

When she called from Meadville, Pennsylvania, she expounded on her love of the Mulligan family and the quaint town that held our family history. "I miss your Dad so much. He would interpret everything for me here. There are so many stories to suss out, and I am writing them all down."

When they finally arrived home in Rhode Island, the group punctuated the journey by breaking the side view mirror of the bus on the telephone pole in front of our house. She seemed happy and relieved that the house was maintained well while she was gone. "Patrick and David were happy to see me," she reported. "They are adults now."

In the early spring of 1977, she called in an agitated and apprehensive tone. "I had to let Pat Kralik go," she blurted when I answered. "Ma," I groaned. "What happened?" "Pat was setting me up and she asked Patrick to take her daughter Missy to school. He said he would, but despite her constant reminders he never did. There's been a lot of tension building up. Pat gave me an ultimatum. She said she could not take care of me as long as Patrick lived here. What could I do? I deserted Patrick once. I could not do it again." Within a week after that call, my mother summoned me home. Her health was deteriorating and she seemed desperate for stability. I had a job at the time and I was taking a full load of courses at UC Santa Cruz. Yet, as I prepared for the journey back to Rhode Island, the uncertainty concerning my life in Monterey didn't seem to matter.

Then I received a call from Michael, while I was still trying to settle my affairs in California. "You'd better hurry, Bernie. We admitted Mom to Rhode Island Hospital. She has a kidney stone the size of a baseball and she is not doing well at all." I dropped my classes, took leave from my job, and immediately jumped on a plane home.

Chapter Forty-Eight - Waiting Room

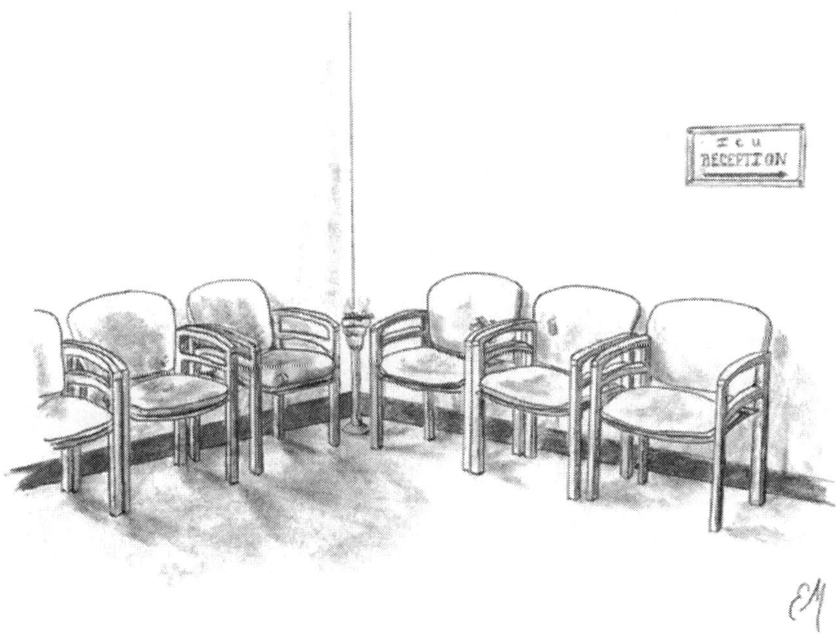

ICU Waiting Room

The ICU waiting room at Rhode Island Hospital was filled with cigarette smoke. Four thick glass ashtrays, cradled in fake bronze stands, smoldered in each corner. Visitors, some crying, reading, or sleeping, occupied the stuffed vinyl chairs. Michael was smoking in a chair that had duct tape holding it together, crisscrossed behind him and flanking his body like tentacles. Wordlessly, Mike stubbed his cigarette out and grasped my arm to pull me down the hall. Had I dreamed of this episode already? It seemed familiar. I could see the room where she lay, surrounded by saline bags, cranking respirators and blinking dials. A bright ray of morning sun cast over my mother's bed. Every dangling wire, tube, and hose in the room converged upon her bed and into her extremities. "God must be in need of suffering," I thought. The initial emotional eruption across my face had no impact upon her countenance. "Ma, when does this all stop?" I asked tearfully. Her eyes were wide open and she followed my movement, but she showed no reaction. I recoiled back, only to catch Michael monitoring my response in a remote, almost clinical manner. He reached for me and pulled me back to the smoke-filled waiting area. As we stood in the middle, surrounded by people in chairs, I could not help but notice the theatrical nature of the room's absurd setting. "We're taking shifts," Michael announced quietly as he gently tapped my arm. "You're up. It's your shift, starting now." The eyes of the entire waiting room were upon us as he delivered his line. The woman seated behind him raised her paperback where she had placed it on her knee, perhaps shielding herself from the tense energy that we were bringing into the already stressed room. I found a seat as far from the fuming ashtrays as possible. Since I was unprepared for sentry duty, I closed my eyes and wondered, "Can I connect with her telepathically?" No sooner had I developed the frame of mind required, when a sudden quiet in the room interrupted my meditation. I opened my eyes and scanned the faces around me. They were all staring into the doorway leading to the nurse's station as a doctor in operating room dress, hands in his pocket, whispered to a young couple. The doctor nodded his head after he imparted the news, and everyone returned to their activities. The young woman evidently affected by the doctor's report slumped back into her chair and eased her head back against the vinyl headrest. Her husband sat beside her. She closed her eyes, squeezing large tears out and down the sides of her face.

Exhausted from my trip, during which I grappled with the images of my mother's suffering, I felt unable to think clearly. I had no emotional reserves left to empathize with or be stimulated by what was happening in the room. I fell into a daze, quickly followed by sleep. "Ma, give me some sign," I pleaded in my dream. She just stared at me, the violent jarring of the respirator giving her movement. I forced myself to wake up. The air had cleared of smoke and the waiting room crowd had dwindled. The young woman who had been crying earlier sat cross-legged, bent over a book of crossword puzzles. I looked at the doorway and wondered if I should venture in again.

A pacemaker had been installed to regulate my mother's heartbeat. The staff spoke to her, but like me, they did not witness any indication that my mother understood or cared. Knowing that she deserved complete honesty, cognizant or not, I had rehearsed my lines. Peering down at her I said, "I suppose you'll be with Dad soon. Are you in pain?" Her eyes met mine; her pupils seemed to be swelling and contracting in concert with the machines. "It is painful for me to see you this way. I will bring some music on my next shift."

When I returned to the waiting room, a new family had arrived. I knew them. Their son, Paul Farley had hired me for $75.00 to help him achieve Conscientious Objector status in order to evade the draft. I had become an expert in the subject during my one year, nine months, and eleven days in the US Army. Now, it was Paul who had been in a terrible car accident and currently occupied a bed in Intensive Care. The Farley's emotions were subdued, punctuated by sniffles and sighs, as they told the story. Other patients' families conveyed their sorrow in demonstrative ways like falling on their knees, imploring God, and wailing against the unfairness of life. "Things were really going well for him," someone commented.

I tried to imagine the faces of all the young people from our neighborhood as they glimpsed cautiously at my mother. Her strength had eased their transition through adolescence and into early adulthood. Swathed entirely in white to hide her gangrenous limbs and the evidence of surgery, Marie's face was all that was left for them to see. Bereft of speech and movement, my mother could not console the young people that needed her. One by one, each member of the "karass" joined me in the waiting room that afternoon. The girls stopped applying eye make-up and their red, tear-swollen eyes became a badge of their grief. Sadly, Michael, Patrick, David, and I did not console one another all that much. We reported on the condition of my mother dutifully at the end of each shift. We did not discuss our feelings. Perhaps, after decades of obeying her demand that we expose our innermost thoughts for discussion and analysis, the ability to maintain our privacy was an unexpected comfort.

Ruth Avenue still existed as a destination for most everyone in the neighborhood, although it operated clumsily due to Marie's hospitalization. Her absence dulled the mood. On one of the last nights at home, I sat on my mother's rocking bed. I asked someone to turn it on. The television at the foot of the bed was showing a commercial, but I could only view it in segments as I went up and down. The pressure on my lungs to open and close at an involuntary cadence caught me by surprise. Eventually, everyone took a turn on the bed. The experience incited tears and laughter. As I sat in the easy chair, I began to think of this spontaneous activity as a new aspect of the polio game that Michael and I had played. Anyone interested in playing would be required to turn the pages of a book with a rubber tipped mouthpiece. Players would also have to memorize the location of every book, every can of food, and every appliance contained in the home. "Remember to number the cupboards and closets," I thought. Everyone would have to be totally still, and not move a muscle for twenty-two years.

Chapter Forty-Nine - Another Day at the Beach

I awoke to the sound of blue jays bickering in the pear tree, and peered out the window to watch them flit back and forth in the gray morning light. I thought of how the pear tree's limbs used to cover the nose of the original Reo Bus. It is just a memory. The date was May 21st, 1977, and I was preparing to fly back to California to save my job and my grade point average. My mother had rebounded. She suddenly began to acknowledge her visitors. She actually smiled at me when I played *Greensleeves* on the little tape deck I had placed at the head of her bed. Dad had always said that the song was insipid enough to cause little or no pain. My mother was thinking of him, I just knew it. Michael and I had confronted her doctors; the irony of their heroic efforts, via surgeries and machines, was that she was confused and in pain. The minute they ceased intervention, her lucidity began to return and the pain diminished. I got out of bed and walked through the house. It was anemic without its rowdy occupants, and felt so strange to me. It seemed like an abandoned carnival; nothing more than chipped paint and clouded mirrors. The numbered cupboards and the lettered closets were, now, useless and inconsequential. In time, 56 Ruth Avenue would harbor some other family and the extraordinary events of our home would be gone.

On my last visit to the hospital, I peeled back the blankets and sheets to expose the body that I knew better than my own. I felt an eerie sense, almost a premonition, as I realized that it was the six-year anniversary of Dad's death. I remembered rubbing her hands to console her after his passing and glanced at them now, curved over supportive pads. However, they were as blue as the day the rescue team first stole her away from my brothers and me. As I touched her cold skin, I recalled the day that the ambulance sped down our street. The neighborhood pulsed with its red light, projecting the rhythm of our broken hearts. I was five years old when she became a person, damaged, with needs that surpassed my own. She was incarcerated, hopelessly, in her own body only sending missives of her love from the dark cell of paralysis. She would never be entirely a mother again, though this did nothing to dampen our intimacy. From the day I first saw her through the hospital window, her head protruding from the iron lung, to the moment she came home in a wheelchair with the chest-piece fastened around her torso, I felt the loss of the physical interaction children crave with their mother. Begrudgingly, I shared her attention with my dad, my brothers, the newspaper people, the vendors, the clergy, the neighbors, and the local children. Recognizing the vacuum left by polio, she gently and lovingly soothed the pain of what I lacked by urging me to express the feelings that might have otherwise been locked inside. "What's wrong, Bernie, where's that smile? Tell me," she would implore. Now, Marie Andree Cooper was dying.

There was no one even remotely like Marie. I did not know anyone who could cry joyfully to the sound of the Beatles singing, "She's Leaving Home". One could not find a more reliable cheerleader. "You are a great writer," she'd proclaim. "You sing wonderfully just like your father," she'd say proudly. Her sincere praise and genuine interest in my talent and intellect strengthened me. I listened to the machines that squawked around us. They seemed feeble compared to her life force. I understood that the love I received outpaced the love that was lost and that she was the most remarkable human I would ever know. Before departing, I glanced at her one more time as she slept, keeping all the things I wanted to say to her in some numbered cupboard of my own. The pain I felt as I left her room was that of a distraught five year old, whose mother was leaving once again.

Marie opened her eyes for the last time. Blinking rapidly, she felt a vapor-like quality to the air, as if the ocean were nearby, and waves were approaching her. She closed her eyes and sunk slowly into the sheets, and then rapidly into the sea. She woke again, as if the hospital had been a dream, and watched bubbles from her first exhalation rise to meet the flickers of light that emanated from all directions. As she submerged deeper and deeper towards the bottom of the ocean, the depth diminished the pressure that paralysis had once exerted upon her body, in a different life. The water filled her lungs allowing her to breathe, she propelled her body upwards. Bursting through the surf, she inhaled the salty air as deeply as she had the ocean water moments before. Expanding her chest, she flipped over on her back to float and watch the fleeting clouds above. Feeling the urge to return to shore, and to walk, she spun over to swim gracefully towards the coast. In her wake, the refuse of machines drifted out with the tide.

Reaching the beach, she ran to the familiar army blanket not far from the waves, picked up her towel, and briskly rubbed her hair. The sand cushioned her feet and she explored the granules with her toes. Bernard sat there staring at the horizon, gripping his pipe. His music books were strewn haphazardly on the sand and on the blanket. Kneeling behind him, she pressed her chest to his back and hugged. "I've made a decision, darling," he said. "I would prefer to stay here, at the beach." Throwing her arms around his neck she giggled, "Let's do, let's do."

Acknowledgements

1) *Rachel Carter*: Rachel was involved as a reader, editor, and writer throughout the entire process. Her originality and love of language was a great help. She frequently became my mother's voice in the drafting process, as her own arduous stay in a hospital allowed her to empathize with Marie's dilemma. She eloquently described for me the tedium associated with prolonged hospital convalescence.

2) *Flora Bates*: Flora urged me to be more descriptive and she introduced me to her mother, Carol Greene.

3) *Carol Greene*: Reader, consultant, talented artist, and friend, whose insight and passion helped me tap into the motivation of the characters. Carol urged me to connect the story to my own feelings without encroaching on the main character: my mother.

4) *Emily McCoomb*: Emily created most of the illustrations and is an honest, but gentle, critic. Her originality and skill is evident throughout the book.

5) *Ed Rooney and Bet Low*: Bet and Ed plowed through Book I, challenging me to alter structure and concepts. By cheering me on and engaging me in lengthy discussions, Bet and Ed proved that good friends are essential to any long-term creative endeavor.

6) *Mimi Kugler*: As my life-partner, Mimi has been encouraging me to discuss this story for twenty-five years. She corrected grammar and syntax and provided unending support.

7) *Joan Kugler*: Mimi's mother, Joan, is an exceptional reader and source of encouragement.

8) *Erin Mulligan*: Erin is a fabulous daughter and sharp reader. Erin also compiled a moving DVD for me of her grandmother from old Super 8 movies.

9) *Jonathan Mulligan*: Jonathan is an insightful reader who would read passages out loud with perfect tone and inflection.

10) *Steve Barao*: Steve Barao is an incredible photographer and great friend, who cleaned up old photographs and is the source of the best post-polio picture of my mother.

11) *Emily Singletary*: Emily is a gentle reader who always made me feel good about the story and my writing skills. Her perspective on the story is unique and useful. She also helped with editing and guarding the latest version diligently.

12) *John O'Neill*: I have known John since Kindergarten and his analysis of the first final draft was critical to the completion of the story.

13) *Ken Dooley*: I have known Ken since Kindergarten, also, and he is a valuable witness and contributor to the events of the story.

14) *Pat Kralik*: Pat is a character in the book, and ours is one of the most important relationships I have ever had. Pat's recollections added drama and humor to the story.

15) *Ann Regan*: My mother depended heavily on Ann for her care. She is such a reliable person and her Rhode Island accent is a special feature of the story.

16) *Kathy Mitchell*: Kathy is a beautiful woman who was instrumental in caring for my mother and lifting everyone's spirits.

17) *Tom Mulligan*: Tom Mulligan consulted with me on the Meadville Pennsylvania perspective. He is a friend and a cousin.

18) *Susan Desorcy*: Susan cared for my mother, and drove the Winnebago to Niagara Falls after having just obtained her driver's license. She was an important witness and one of the original members of the green stamp production brigade.

19) *Cindy Desorcy*: Cindy was a friend and helper to my mother. Marie enjoyed her intelligent company immensely.

20) *Sal Traverse*: Driver of the Winnebago, who took on substantial responsibility for the mechanical health of the massive vehicle. Sal is a great artist, musician, and friend. He contributed his art to the book.

21) *Kate Roberts*: Kate is a source of inspiration and she contributed the photo of 509 10th Street.

22) *Kayla Hood*: First reader who helped me initiate the book

23) *Kathy Rook*: Kept me company during the most trying times of my life.

24) *Amber Zucker*: My good friend in Tulsa who read my book and offered valuable insight.

25) *Andy Heald*: A good army friend who read the book in two days and bolstered my confidence with his comments.

26) *Roy Call*: Great army friend who drove the Winnebago over treacherous roads much to the glee of my mother.

27) *Sister James Francis*: My aunt was the witness to my father's childhood and the chronicler of the rich Mulligan history. She also contributed financially.

28) *Erica Sahlin*: Erica's insight into the layout and content helped me focus on the final draft

29) *Michael Mulligan*: Michael and I had many incredible conversations recounting our lives as his was coming to an end.

30) *The Karass*: Bill Hanson, Doreen Guy, Johnny Guy, Heather Kralik, Missy Kralik, Margaret Rook, Alisha, Ray Morrissey (Ray the Mailman), Phyllis Gentile, Stephan Gentile, Phillip Gentile, Eddie Desorcy, Joan Regan, Joe Regan, Billy Regan, Elisha Macready, Ray Francis, Susan Francis, Tom Francis, Vinnie Francis, Sharon McNulty, Linda Desorcy, Kathy Garrity, Beverley Nelson, Denise Daly, Bruce Doull, Kathy Ward, Jeanie Ward, Manny Fonseca, Gary Carter, Jimmy Regan, Mary Regan, and many others who loved Marie Andree Cooper.

31) *Coffee Depot:* A special thanks to the beautiful women at the Depot who kept me going with their cheerfulness and caffeine.

32) *Eden Castro:* is an insightful and compassionate reader who also helped me with the book's format and arrangement. She offered kind inspiration.

33) *Natasha Fields:* An excellent reader from Tulsa who fell in love with my mother and offered valuable insight into the narrative

34) *Ashley Dawn Fuller:* Ashley's perspective on the questions we

have of our mothers caused me to reflect on what I do not know about Marie

35) *Kathy Obrien:* Kathy edited the book with great skill and patience. She is a childhood friend who attended St. Margaret's School.

36) *Maddie Dennis:* Maddie is a very talented artist who finished the illustration. She also read the book and made some excellent suggestions

37) *Mary Elizabeth Perreira:* Compassionate reader and artist

38) *Cathy Scanlon:* Reader who urged to me to include vignettes of Marie's early life

39) *Eric Mancini:* Eric is a talented author and gifted writer who handled production and final editing.

Thank you Marie

Made in the USA
Columbia, SC
27 September 2017